VOL

THE SEARCH

CANO

FOR VESUVIUS

WILLIAM HOFFER

SUMMIT BOOKS
NEW YORK

Published by SUMMIT BOOKS
A Simon & Schuster Division of Gulf & Western Corporation
Simon & Schuster Building
Rockefeller Center
1230 Avenue of the Americas
New York, New York 10020
SUMMIT BOOKS and colophon
are trademarks of Simon & Schuster
Designed by Edith Fowler
Manufactured in the United States of America

10 9 8 7 6 5 4 3 2 1
First Edition

Library of Congress Cataloging in Publication Data

Hoffer, William.
    Volcano: the search for Vesuvius.

    Bibliography: p.
    1. Vesuvius (Italy) 2. Vesuvius (Italy)—History.
I. Title.
QE523.V5H63   945'.73   81-23325
ISBN 0-671-40079-7   AACR2

To Marilyn

CONTENTS

PREFACE

THE ERUPTION of Mount St. Helens in the spring of 1980 intruded into our tidy technological world and reminded us that nature has little concern for our pretensions. We would prefer to associate an erupting volcano with ancient history, not with these last decades of the twentieth century.

But few who viewed that volcanic ash cloud, which so closely resembled the mushroom of an atomic explosion, could fail to recall another famous volcanic event, the eruption of Mount Vesuvius that destroyed Pompeii over nineteen hundred years ago. As one reporter put it:

> Geologists estimate that St. Helens spewed out about 1.5 cubic miles of debris, a blast on about the same order of magnitude as the one in A.D. 79 from Italy's Vesuvius, which buried Pompeii and Herculaneum with ash and mud.

Vesuvius and Mount St. Helens are separated by seven thousand miles and by a great disparity in the countryside they overshadow. Mount St. Helens is a wilderness volcano, venting itself mainly on the forest, the animals, the rivers and lakes. Vesuvius dominates one of the most densely populated areas in Western civilization.

They pose somewhat different threats, but both volcanoes reveal man's confusing reaction to this phenomenon. Why, we might ask, do Americans live within range of a volcanic chain that runs through Mount Rainier, Mount Hood, Lassen Peak and the still-fulminating Mount St. Helens? Why do millions continue to make their homes within deadly proximity to Mount Vesuvius? What prompts a people who have been devastated by numerous eruptions from Vesuvius during the past three centuries to repeatedly rebuild on top of the lava?

The answer seems to be a human spirit sometimes called indomitable, other times viewed as foolhardy. In either case, it is one that stubbornly insists that man will someday tame the natural forces. If not for this, we might still be living in caves, seeking protection from the elements.

The history of Vesuvius is a microcosm of that contest between man and his environment, a story that includes a frightening series of catastrophes better documented than those of any other volcano. The drama involves lost cities, buried treasure and those who sought to uncover a forgotten past.

Vesuvius is also the centerpiece of a larger history, through which run the variables of warfare, religion, politics, archaeology, science, love, greed and superstition. The lives of celebrated characters intersect the volcano: the slave-general Spartacus, the Roman admiral and naturalist Pliny the Elder, the mystical martyr San Gennaro, the strange love trio of Britain's Sir William Hamilton, his Lady Emma and Lord Horatio Nelson. Writers Goethe, Shelley, Dickens and Twain walked its slopes, often in danger, and described the volcano to an intrigued world.

This is the story of the volcano's future as well, and with it the future of all who are threatened by its capricious nature. It led me from Front Royal, Virginia, to Naples, Italy, to the top of the volcano, more than five hundred feet down into its crater, then across the Italian countryside in search of the secrets of civilized man's most unusual neighbor.

"It must be admitted that Vesuvius revealed itself to the world by a master stroke. To cover land and sea with a black cloud; to send its ashes as far afield as Africa, Syria, and Egypt; to bury two cities like Pompeii and Herculaneum; to asphyxiate, over a distance of a mile, a philosopher like Pliny, and to have his nephew record the catastrophe by means of an immortal letter—you will grant that this is not bad at all for a volcano that is only just setting out on its career. . . ."

ALEXANDRE DUMAS, *père,*
author of *The Three Musketeers*
and Director of Excavations
at Pompeii and Herculaneum,
1860.

ITALY

• Rome

AREA OF
DETAIL MAP

Naples

SEA
OF
TYRRHENIA

SICILY

Massa di Somma

San Sebastiano

Santa Anastasia

Monte Nuovo
La Solfatara

San Giorgio
a Cremano

Somma Vesuviana

NAPLES

Cercola

Mount Somma

Ottaviano

Cuma

Baia

Pozzuoli

Portici

VESUVIUS

San Giuseppe

Ercolano

Resina
(Herculaneum)

Terzigno

Misenum

Torre del Greco

Boscoreale

Boscotrecase

ISCHIA

Torre Annunziata

Pompeii

Castellammare
di Stabia

BAY OF NAPLES

SEA OF TYRRHENIA

CAPRI

Sorrento

Punta della Campanella

N

Vesuvius and the
Bay of Naples

5   10   15
MILES

Cal Sacks

1

THE SEARCH FOR VESUVIUS

My journey to Vesuvius began on a summer afternoon at the Museum of Fine Arts in Boston, Massachusetts. We were closely packed into a darkened gallery, for this was the next to the last day of a special exhibition commemorating the nineteen hundredth anniversary of the destruction of Pompeii by the eruption of Vesuvius on August 24, A.D. 79. The show was on loan from the Italian National Museum at Naples.

I was drawn toward a glass display case in which something hideous, yet entrancing, was entombed. It was the ghost-white mold of a young Pompeiian woman who perished with thousands of her fellow villagers in the eruption. She was lying upon her stomach, her legs crimped slightly, her brow resting upon her right forearm, her fist clenched in resolution, or perhaps convulsion. Her hair was clipped short, her tunic gathered up above the waistline, leaving the lower half of her body nude. Not an attractive image of one's death, I thought, to choke on poisonous fumes, only to have your agony bared to the public some two thousand years later.

The museum program said that this body cast was a copy lent to the exhibit by Imperial Tobacco Limited. The original was still at Pompeii. The original what?

As gruesome as the woman was the dog unearthed in the house of Vesonius Primus, who lived on the northern edge of Pompeii. The cast of the animal's body showed him looped into a fetal position, his head upside down, as though straining against a devilish force. His muzzle was half-open in palpable pain. He still wore his collar, the studs starkly visible.

•

The museum program explained how the image was preserved:

> The unfortunate dog, wearing his bronze-studded collar, was left chained up, and he suffocated beneath the ash and cinders. These then hardened round the corpse, forming an impression that, with the disintegration of the organic remains, became a perfect hollow mold. It was the archaeologist Fiorelli who first realized that by filling such hollow molds with plaster one could obtain faithful replicas of objects such as bodies, wooden doors, furniture and foodstuffs.

These death casts are among the most extraordinary products of archaeology. Their creator, Giuseppe Fiorelli, a nineteenth-century director of the excavations at Pompeii, immediately recognized that while marble statuary and the shells of grandiose villas would be helpful in reconstructing Pompeiian life, nothing would depict the agony of the town's destruction as well as these somber plaster impressions that froze the moment when life was extinguished.

I was curious about that moment. Did the Pompeiians know what was happening to them, or did they slip into eternity with the unanswerable lingering in their final thoughts?

Examining the museum program I learned that there had been a dramatic warning, that Pompeii had been shattered by a severe earthquake on February 5, A.D. 62, which was caused by an aborted eruption of Vesuvius. Seventeen years later, when the volcano finally annihilated the Roman city, only two of its great public buildings, the Temple of Isis and the Amphitheatre, had been totally rebuilt.

But if the earthquake was so enormous, why hadn't the Pompeiians migrated to a safer, nonvolcanic area? Here is evidence that human understanding evolves slowly. Two millennia later millions still choose to live astride California's San Andreas fault.

I abandoned the thought and drifted toward the other displays of Pompeii's past. There were numerous glass cases filled with jewelry, some found in the final grasp of a victim. Nearby was the reconstruction of a Pompeiian garden from the House of Menander, thought to have belonged to the family of Nero's wife, Poppaea Sabina. Life was obviously pleasant there, at least prior to the volcanic Judgment Day.

I eased out of the crowded museum halls to a side room where only a few people quietly milled. Along the walls was a secondary exhibit of volcanic art. Most of the paintings depicted anonymous or fanciful volcanoes, but several showed Vesuvius itself. Pompeii was merely the effect; here was the cause. One canvas showed a night view from the Bay of Naples in which the summit of Vesuvius glowed with a rich red fire. Golden meteors burst from the crater and splashed into the bay, where boiling waters mirrored the Stygian panorama. "Vesuvius in Eruption, 1872," the caption read.

1872? I was startled. The volcanic eruption that buried Pompeii in A.D. 79 was the only one I was aware of, but apparently there had been a devastating explosion of Vesuvius little more than one hundred years ago. In geological terms nineteen hundred years is barely the flick of an eye. If Vesuvius had erupted only one hundred years ago it surely retained the potential to threaten one of the most populous regions of Western civilization. I resolved to learn more about the great volcano.

A few weeks later, Dr. Tom Simkin, curator of petrology and volcanology at the Smithsonian Institution's National Museum of Natural History in Washington, D.C., met me in the museum's central hall and shook my hand with a vigor that caused his long brown ponytail to move up and down. We walked through a hallway of dinosaur skeletons, up a curving stairway, into an office crowded with technical journals. Simkin listened with interest as I told him of my visit to Boston's Museum of Fine Arts and my surprise in learning that Vesuvius had erupted in 1872.

"People know that Vesuvius destroyed Pompeii," he explained. "But they know little else about the rest of its history, which is plentiful. Vesuvius is the most active volcano on the mainland of Europe. It has been in a frequent state of eruption for the past three hundred years."

Vesuvius has a known history of eruptions dating back several thousand years, Simkin explained. Since the Pompeiian eruption of A.D. 79 it has exploded violently dozens of times, though there is little documentation prior to a devastating eruption in 1631. There are excellent records of its activity during the past 350 years that show that each major eruption has been followed by cycles of dormancy. After each dormant period came years of mild activity culminating in still another cataclysmic explosion.

"Has it exploded since 1872?" I asked.

"Yes. There have been several large eruptions since then. The first was in 1906. The last was in 1944, a few months after the Allied armies occupied Naples. The eruption emptied out the crater of Vesuvius and destroyed villages on the slopes."

"Has anything happened since then?"

The volcanologist pondered. "It's been quiet, but it's really been a very short period of time in a geologic sense. To say that Vesuvius hasn't erupted since 1944 means very little. The odds are certainly high that it could become active again at any time."

I left Simkin's office burdened with unanswered questions, which months of study and discussions with volcanologists gradually crystallized into one gnawing conundrum: How does humanity coexist with a live volcano?

The question came into focus late one night as I drove to the Blue Ridge Mountains of Virginia and climbed the back country roads to my home on Dickey Ridge, just north of Chester Gap. I mused about Appalachia's own volcanic heritage. The mountains I live in were created by a series of violent volcanic upheavals during the Precambrian Period, between 570 million and 1.1 billion years ago. Today they rest in serene maturity, worn smooth by eons of erosion, now covered with dense deciduous forests that are evidence of the comfortable remoteness of Appalachia's volcanic history.

But Vesuvius and the system to which it belongs are geologically much younger, more active and more threatening to man's carefully developed environment. I was living safely in the comfort of ancient, spent volcanoes while more than two million Italians, including the congested populace of Naples, are within the fatal range of a volcano that has erupted as recently as 1944. Half a million have settled at the very base of Vesuvius in villages whose foundations are composed of layers of lava, pumice, ash and other products left as geologic souvenirs from the volcano's frequent eruptions.

The residents were reminded of the peril on November 23, 1980, when an earthquake devastated the countryside, killing more than three thousand people. The epicenter of the quake was near the village of Battipaglia, thirty miles south of Vesuvius. The destruction was worst in the southern portions of the region, but damage was also severe closer to Vesuvius and beyond. The people looked uneasily to Vesuvius, for even the least sophisticated farmer is aware that earthquakes and volcanic eruptions are closely related.

Portions of the Pompeii ruins were destroyed once again, and for a time the city had to be closed to tourists. In Naples, nearly forty miles from the epicenter, tens of thousands were left homeless, forced to evacuate their crowded apartments for fear that the weakened structures would collapse. Even the city's elegant hotels closed their upper floors to guests.

The entire area surrounding Vesuvius, a region known as Campania, is a place of paradox. To the Romans it was Campania Felix—"The Happy Land." At the height of the republic it served as a resort area to such rich Romans as Lucullus and Cicero, who had villas at Pompeii, Cumae and Puteoli, modern Pozzuoli. The home of Emperor Claudius, near the present site of Boscotrecase, belonged to the previous emperor, Tiberius, and possibly to Augustus, earlier still.

Campanians enjoy warm sea winds that flow year-round from the Mediterranean north toward Naples. The winter season is brief and snow a curiosity, even though Naples is as far north of the equator as New York City. The climate is as providential today as it was two thousand years ago when the Roman poet Statius declared: "All things conspire to make life pleasant in the land, where the summers are cool and winters warm, and where the sea dies away gently as it kisses the shore."

The climate enables farmers to grow three, occasionally four, crops a year of apricots, olives, lemons and wine grapes. Vesuvius has helped shape the gracious aspect of this land, its eruptions having crafted much of Campania's contours into a soil made rich by decomposed volcanic debris.

Yet a curse is buried within the earth that seems so hospitable. Geologists call Campania a "crib area," a countryside undermined by multiple "faults," subterranean cracks in the earth's crust, one of which runs north and south from a point near Rome, then close to Naples through Pompeii itself. Over the past two millennia this fault has bedeviled the Happy Land with earth shocks and volcanic explosions.

At a point almost midway between Naples and Pompeii, the north-south fault, called Lineation 15, intersects a second fault, which runs from a point near Vesuvius through the volcano, then westward to the seaside town of Torre del Greco. It is at the precise juncture of these two faults that the central cone of Vesuvius rises to dominate the landscape. This is the point of greatest danger, but no part of Campania is immune to the earth faults below it or the volcanic crater above it.

It is a testimony to human stubbornness that anyone lives in Campania at all. It would not have been surprising if after the fall of Pompeii the people had forsaken the land forever. But even though the volcano has exploded scores of times since A.D. 79, the people keep returning to the slopes of the mountain, even to rebuild new towns closer to Vesuvius than Pompeii itself. In 1631, when Vesuvius flooded nearby Torre del Greco with boiling watery lava, killing more people than died at Pompeii, the villagers rebuilt the town, as modern Campanians have continued to do.

I decided to go to Naples to find out why, and to investigate the volcano that popular misinformation has so long portrayed as being as extinct as the Roman cities it had once destroyed.

2

A VISIT TO THE VOLCANO

It WAS 5:30 A.M. in Naples, Italy. My sense of time was upset by the protracted trip: a flight from Washington to New York, a layover at Kennedy, an eight-hour overnighter to Rome, another layover, finally the short flight to Naples. In all, it was nineteen hours plus a six-hour time zone difference. I should have felt exhausted, but my scurrying mind precluded sleep.

Six stories below the balcony of my room at the Hotel Vesuvio, Naples was awakening. Midget cars moved along the Via Partenope past fishing boats rocking at their moorings in a small marina opposite my hotel. In the rare moments when traffic subsided, I could hear the bay waters slapping against the crumbling walls of the Castle Ovo. As freighters slept offshore, the first ferryboat from the island of Capri edged silently toward the commercial dockyards.

Eight miles to the southeast, Mount Vesuvius rose to greet the morning. The mountain stood mute, but its authority was unquestionable. There was no smoke, no sign of its inherent ability to sear the countryside, yet I knew that I was staring at the most active volcano on the mainland of Europe. Nowhere else on earth is there such a historic geologic threat in intimate proximity to a busy metropolis.

I felt a compelling certainty that Vesuvius was alive, and not merely in the sense that its chambers housed masses of the deadly mixture of gas and molten rock known as magma. The feeling was more intense, an irrational fear that the volcano was teasing the Neapolitans as it had the Pompeiians prior to August 24, A.D. 79.

I had arrived the previous afternoon on an Alitalia DC-9,

from which I could see one of the world's superior natural harbors, the crescent-shaped Bay of Naples that stretches across more than twenty miles on the west coast of the Italian peninsula. Its huddled towns created a continuous serpentine from Naples to Sorrento that appeared to be one city from the air.

I had been introduced to Vesuvius as my plane circled on its landing approach. Vesuvius seemed gentle from a distance, sloping out lazily on all sides, its twin summits reminiscent of a double-humped "Bactrian" camel. Up close it was unmistakably a volcano that had disrupted the peace of the land, its reddish-brown upper slopes splashed with streams of black lava twisting fingerlike down the mountain.

The rim of the larger, four-thousand-foot-high central cone, generally referred to as "Vesuvius," hinted at the deep volcanic crater that lay inside. A mile behind rose the second peak known as Mount Somma, about thirty-six hundred feet. Somma is not really a mountain in its own right, but a curving ridge that is all that remains of a cone that was once half again as high as the present Vesuvius. This ancient giant was probably the Vesuvius the Pompeiians knew.

I was impatient to visit the volcano, to walk the mountain that for centuries has dominated the Campanians. My first destination was the Osservatorio Vesuviana, where I was to speak with Dr. Giuseppe Luongo, professor of physical volcanology at the University of Naples, the man charged with the daily surveillance of Vesuvius.

Driving south from Naples, we reached the village of Torre del Greco where Vesuvius loomed three miles ahead. We began the ascent slowly, negotiating a series of blind S-curves up the mountain, along a low stone wall that shielded us from the steep drop. One moment the peak stood above us, then abruptly we were facing out in the other direction over a panorama of Naples.

Halfway up the mountain, we passed the faded Hotel Eremo, then approached an imposing three-story red-brick structure topped by a belfry. It was the old observatory building, the world's first permanent volcanic monitoring station, now used mainly to house seismic equipment. The new observatory, a modern concrete structure, was a short distance farther along the mountain on the same road.

In the large hall of the observatory, where students sat studying at conference tables, I met Luongo's assistant, Vincent D'Arreco, who haltingly told me that Doctor Luongo would soon arrive to speak with me, in English. While we waited, Vincent showed me a polychrome wall map that illustrated the volcanic structure of Italy, its legend indicating that the color brown represented volcanic ground.

Vincent's index finger traced the eastern edge of Sicily. "Etna," he declared. He then slid up to an arc of brown dots off the northern coast of Sicily. "Ustica, Alicudi, Filicudi, Lipari, Vulcano, Panarea, Stromboli." I was familiar with Etna and Stromboli, and Vulcano had obviously conferred its name upon the entire category, but I did not know there were so many volcanoes in Italy. Vincent pointed to a circular brown spot in the Apennine Mountains representing a volcano named Vultari, then traced a path to a large patch of brown eight miles southeast of Naples.

"Vesuvio," he emphasized.

His finger continued north and west of Naples, locating La Solfatara, Monte Nuovo and eleven extinct volcanoes in the area known as the Phlegraean ("Fiery") Fields, and Mount Epomeo on the offshore island of Ischia. Rome itself was surrounded by several volcanic craters, among them the present sites of Lake Bolsena and Lake Bracciano.

Vincent then drew me to a cross-sectional map of Vesuvius, encompassing the area from the village of Santa Anastasia on the north-northwest to the ruins of Pompeii on the south-southeast. Mount Somma, 3,622 feet high at the loftiest elevation of its curving ridge, drops precipitously on the side facing the central cone, forming the deep channels known as the Atrio del Cavallo and the Valley of the Inferno. The land then slopes upward to the peak of Vesuvius, 4,035 feet high. The hollow dish of the crater drops 525 feet, from the lowest point of the rim. But physical statistics for Vesuvius are impermanent; large portions of the volcanic cone periodically fall inward after each eruption, gradually eroding the summit.

I asked Vincent if he was apprehensive about working on the slopes of Vesuvius. "No," he answered confidently. "The volcano is dormant."

Vincent turned as Dr. Luongo, a dark-complected man, strode energetically through the entranceway. We spoke in Dr. Luongo's office on the second floor where Vincent waited deferentially in the doorway. "I have talked with Tom Simkin at the Smithsonian Institution in Washington," I informed Luongo. "He suggested that I speak with the volcanologists here at Vesuvius. Tom tells me Vesuvius is alive, but Vincent has just told me that it's dormant."

Luongo looked at Vincent piercingly, then spoke rapidly to him in Italian as the younger man listened with a chastised expression. "We have trouble with this problem," Luongo explained. "Too many in Naples misunderstand. Perhaps 90 percent of the people do not know that this is an active volcano.

"We have a new way of looking at geology today. We look at geologic systems. Vesuvius is part of the same system as Etna and Stromboli, and the Apennine Mountains. If any part of the system is active, then the whole system is active. For years Vesuvius gave us clear warning of danger. It has been quiet since 1944, but that is not necessarily good. From 1631 to 1944 Vesuvius was in continuous activity with a maximum repose period of seven years. This has totally changed."

The observatory now concentrates on scientific surveillance of the volcano for signs of imminent action. Four seismic stations are embedded in the earth of the northern slope of Vesuvius, connected by cable to the observatory. Three form a precise equilateral triangle with the fourth at its center, a configuration that allows Luongo, by triangulation, to pinpoint the origin of each earth shock beneath Vesuvius.

In recent years there have been two peaks of earthquake activity under the volcano, one in 1964, and again in 1974, when some twenty subterranean quakes occurred in the space of minutes. Their intensity was not major, but the rapidity of the shocks has left observers uneasy.

Ground movement has also been observed, a factor monitored by twenty square concrete pillars that rise three feet above the ground, hidden from curious tourists. Twice a year, in the middle of the night, laser beams flash back and forth across the summit measuring alternations in ground level, using the concrete posts as benchmarks. A small dilation of the ground on the western slope, along the faultline that runs directly through Torre del Greco, has been observed, but it is inconclusive.

"Would you like to see the view from the top of Vesuvius?" I nodded assent, and we were soon driving on the black pavement up toward the top of Vesuvius.

"That is called Calle Umberto," Luongo said, indicating a wooded hill created by eruptions in the late nineteenth century. The calle sat upslope from the observatory, protecting it from any lava that would flow from the central cone.

Luongo gestured to the left. "And this valley is the Atrio del Cavallo." This natural trough between the central cone and Mount Somma rises gently parallel to the roadway. The Atrio del Cavallo, or "Hall of the Horse," is now barren and black with lava from the 1944 eruption, but during the eighteenth century it was covered with vegetation. Tourists grazed their horses there while they climbed to the crater on foot, a practice that gave the Atrio its now inappropriate name. On the opposite side, Luongo explained, the continuation of this land formation is called "Valle dell' Inferno," the Valley of the Inferno.

A short distance up from the observatory, Luongo halted the car near a river of black stone that stretched as far as I could see. The lava stream was at least two hundred yards wide, flowing without motion to the lower end of the Atrio. As we continued our drive upward, Luongo indicated the point where the 1944 lava flow, here only fifty feet wide, had funneled through a narrow pass near the top of the Atrio.

"It is possible to put a dam here to save the villages below," Luongo said. "If we have another lava flow from this point, as in 1944, a dam would hold the lava. Unfortunately, in Italy we have no law allowing us to change natural phenomena. By protecting one place we may be destroying another."

Moments later, we arrived at a fork, the right side of which led to a chairlift for tourists who preferred to ride to the summit. On foot, we took the left fork, moving uphill toward the crater along a sinuous path scraped into the russet earth. The hike covered a vertical distance of 650 feet, but its true length easily quadrupled as the path frequently turned back upon itself. The wind lashed my face and pierced the light jacket I wore.

As we talked, Luongo and I continued to walk toward the Bay with Naples below us. From here we had a postcard vista of the bay curling inward in a graceful half-circle. The Bay of Naples begins where the Cape of Misenum juts into the Sea of Tyrrhenia to form a natural defense post, where the Romans had once anchored their fleets. From Misenum the shoreline turns north briefly, forming a spit of land surrounding Lake Avernus where, according to Virgil's *Aeneid*, Hercules communed with the dead.

The coastline then swivels east, fashioning a miniharbor within the bay, centering upon the town of Pozzuoli, the birthplace of Sophia Loren and once a prominent Roman port. Where Pozzuoli ends, Naples begins, a crescent huddled alongside the bay. South of the city, the bay gradually becomes an extended horseshoe encompassing the communities of San Giorgio a Cremano, Portici, Ercolano (Herculaneum), and Torre del Greco. Luongo explained that just as many villages encircle the other sides of the mountain, but Mount Somma blocked our view.

"Where is Pompeii?" I asked.

"You can't see it from here. It is directly across from where we are, to the south," Luongo answered.

The great cone of Vesuvius hid the southern vista where, in addition to the ruins of Pompeii, the villages of Terzigno, Boscoreale, Boscotrecase and Torre dell' Annunziata clustered on the volcano's lower slopes. Further south is Castellammare di Stabia, where Pliny the Elder succumbed during the great eruption of A.D. 79. The shoreline finally turns toward the exquisite resort of Sorrento, the beginning of the Amalfi Drive. Just beyond Sorrento, the Bay of Naples ends at Punta della Campanella.

Luongo and I soon drew alongside the old observatory building, which stood out on a small rise. Directly below us lay what seemed like a frozen gray metallic lake several hundred feet across.

"Is that more lava?" I asked.

"No, it is a pyroclastic flow from the 1944 eruption."

The word means "formed by fire," Luongo explained. A pyroclastic flow may be the most dangerous of all volcanic phenomena. When the requisite mixture of magma and gas is produced, a volcano ejects molten rock upward. Heavier than ash or pumice, the rock is not carried off by the winds, but falls on the upper slopes of the mountain. The heated rocks are so saturated with volatile gases that if struck with a hammer they would explode. This blend of molten rock and gas, not unlike Biblical fire and brimstone, races down the mountainside at sixty miles per hour or more, decimating everything in its path.

A British family, touring the mountain, overheard my conversation with Luongo and politely interrupted.

"If it erupts . . . ?" the woman asked hesitantly.

"Are there signs first?" her husband added.

"It is different depending upon the time between eruptions," Luongo hedged in response. "Now it is a long time between eruptions. In this case we have earthquakes before an eruption, shocks, to open the vent."

We continued upward to a twenty-foot-wide plateau at the summit of Vesuvius where I looked out over the crater, experiencing a sense of disembodiment. Across from me a half dozen steam jets called "fumaroles" wafted upward forming a nebulous curtain. We were at the low side of the crater that is accessible to visitors. The remaining three-fourths of the oval is a higher jagged wall, built up in part by layers of lava and ash from the 1944 eruption.

I peered over the edge of the crater, careful of my footing, for there was no restraining fence. There was a sheer drop of forty feet, then a long slope of loose rock angled at forty-five degrees that stretched to the bottom of the crater. The low point was eccentric, closer to the far wall than to the midpoint. Here and there I could spot a fumarole, but the crater was deep enough to obscure detail. While most of the crater seemed composed of loose stone, two areas, one to my left and one to my right, were covered with slides of reddish-brown volcanic ash. Images of death and destruction raced through my mind. The entire vista was that of a giant vortex sucking stones into the earth.

Luongo and I walked silently back to the top of the pathway, edging past clusters of tourists. Young boys stood at the crater's edge, tossing small stones into the air and watching as they floated down. Now more than ever I felt compelled to understand the great volcano. A fresh thought occurred to me.

"Is it possible to climb into the crater?" I asked Luongo.

"It is possible. Some of the people from the Alpine Club went down last year. But it is very dangerous."

"Have you ever been down?"

"No." He laughed.

"Do you want to go?" I asked.

"No!" He laughed harder. "Do you?"

I pondered the question, but I was not ready to respond. As we stood at the rim, the black river of lava from the 1944 eruption lay below us, arching into the Atrio del Cavallo, tracing a path down to the valley between Vesuvius and Mount Somma. At the lower end of the Atrio the lava tumbled over a sharp precipice and disappeared from view.

"What is below the precipice?" I asked.

"The village of San Sebastiano," Luongo replied softly. "It was almost completely destroyed by the 1944 eruption, but it has been rebuilt."

From this height it was easy to see that the narrow channel of the Atrio del Cavallo would funnel any lava flow from the edge of the crater directly over the precipice onto the land below.

"It doesn't make sense," I said. "Why would anyone live there? It looks like the most vulnerable location in the area."

Luongo shrugged. "San Sebastiano has been destroyed four times," he said. "But it doesn't seem to make any difference. Each time the people come back."

3

CITY OF LAVA

DR. LUONGO'S COMMENT that San Sebastiano had been engulfed by Vesuvius four times made me think of its extraordinary inhabitants, men and women who each time have rebuilt
a new city on top of the old. Are these villagers especially
tenacious, or merely reckless, I wondered? How could they
live under the constant threat of destruction and why, when
the specter became reality, did they insist on returning to this
piece of shaking earth?

I knew that in San Sebastiano there existed evidence of the
strategies by which men and women have survived an active
volcano over the ages, and I set off to visit these resilient
people.

San Sebastiano is six miles southeast of Naples and less than
two miles north of the central crater of Vesuvius. To reach the
village from Naples we exited the autostrada at San Giorgio a
Cremano, then drove inland, always aiming for the valley between the twin peaks of Vesuvius. San Sebastiano sits at the
intersection of the bases of the volcano, below the natural
channel formed by the Atrio del Cavallo. It is an easy target
for Vesuvius.

Since the early nineteenth century, nearly every generation
has seen this village destroyed by the volcano. The first onslaught was on October 27, 1822, when a volcanic mudslide
flowed over the precipice and smothered San Sebastiano so
quickly that the residents had no time to save their possessions. The survivors resolutely rebuilt the village, and for
thirty-three years Vesuvius ignored San Sebastiano.

In 1855 a stream of Vesuvian lava followed the course of the

31

previous mudslide and once again obliterated San Sebastiano. Refusing to relocate, the prideful villagers constructed a new community on the site of the old. Seventeen years later, in 1872, Vesuvius sent another river of molten rock down through the Atrio del Cavallo and across San Sebastiano, destroying the village. Once again the residents rebuilt. On the night of March 21, 1944, San Sebastiano was ravaged for the fourth time by Vesuvius, demolishing two-thirds of the long-suffering town.

The inland towns of Campania generally exhibit a poorer countenance than those that border the Bay of Naples, but modern San Sebastiano is an exception. San Sebastiano is a new town, much of it built directly over the lava that destroyed its three predecessors. It provides a different face from the rotting, multifamily shacks of Santa Anastasia or Terzigno, boasting new villas and apartments of clean architectural line and an abundance of trees, which is rare in an Italian village. On its main street, Via Roma, a series of modern boutiques front upon a red tile sidewalk.

One feature of the town struck me as quite curious. Several streets near the center of town are twenty feet lower than the houses on either side and I had to crane my neck to see the new apartments, which were built in a pattern resulting from the eruption of 1944. Afterward, narrow swaths were cut through the lava to create roadways, while the houses and apartments were simply built on top of the lava, giving them the appearance of sitting on a ledge. As of the most recent census, this unusual village was home to 7,045 people.

Past the silver-domed cathedral of San Sebastiano Martire is a side street bordered by a high stone wall fashioned from blocks of lava. At various points, gates opened onto landscaped courtyards planted with apricot and lemon trees, ferns, palms, pines and cacti.

The municipal offices are located in a new building at the southern edge of town. I asked to speak with someone about the story of the town's recurring destruction and rebirth, and was told to speak with Raffaele Capasso, the mayor. He was home ill, but one of his aides volunteered to drive me to the mayor's house at #46 Via Panoramica Fellapane, "Avenue of the Panorama of a Loaf of Bread." At his modern home set amidst well-cultivated vegetation, the mayor greeted me warmly.

Mayor Capasso was a slim man in his fifties, dressed entirely in brown—sweater, slacks, slippers. As we spoke about Vesuvius, he would pause in his narrative to light a cigarette, which he held from underneath, between his forefinger and middle finger, waving it in the air for emphasis.

Capasso recounted the story of the 1944 eruption with clarity and detail. He was nineteen in 1944 when his village was destroyed by the volcano. The Allies had finally conquered Naples on October 3, 1943, and placed the city under the jurisdiction of the Allied Control Commission, which acted quickly to stabilize life in war-torn Naples.

By the early months of 1944, the Neapolitans dared to dream of normalcy. The one thing they needed least was activity from inside Vesuvius. But at 4:30 P.M. on Saturday, March 18, 1944, the volcano exploded with a roar greater than that of the artillery fire which had scarred its slopes a few months earlier. Red-orange lava poured out over the cone on the northeastern slope and surged into the Atrio del Cavallo where, obstructed by the ridge of Mount Somma, it turned north following the natural channel between the two peaks and descended in the direction of San Sebastiano.

The next day, Sunday, March 19, 1944, Raffaele recalled, his father, Michele Capasso, took him and his brother Vincenzo up the mountain to investigate. Climbing a wooded path south of town that leads up a sharp two-hundred-foot precipice, they gazed up the Atrio del Cavallo to the summit of Vesuvius. They were shocked at the volume of smoking lava that filled the five-hundred-foot width of the Atrio.

The lava oozed along the top of the hardened residue from the eruption of 1872, its leading edge building to a fifteen-foot crest. Instead of flowing at a uniform pace, the lava moved spasmodically, its forward wall cooling and crusting until the inertia of the boiling mass behind it forced it over the top and pushed it ahead with the sound of metal grinding upon metal. Dark scum rode along the luminous surface of the flow.

Many residents of San Sebastiano were confident that any lava flow would collect in the Atrio del Cavallo basin and halt before it reached the precipice above town. But the Capassos were witnesses to the reality: The mass of lava was far greater than anyone had supposed. Certain that it would soon cascade down upon their home, they rushed back to San Sebastiano.

After warning their neighbors, they loaded their few possessions onto a wobbly cart and, without an animal to pull it, Michele Capasso moved between the staves and dragged the cart back and forth between San Sebastiano and the village of Pollena-Trocchia. The village, where the Capassos had relatives, was to the north of San Sebastiano and out of the line of immediate danger.

But San Sebastiano was totally exposed to Vesuvius. That Sunday morning in 1944 the villagers had only their trust in God to protect them. As a black cloud of ash punctuated by lightning hovered overhead, they prayed to San Gennaro, the patron saint of Naples, parading his sacred statue through the narrow lanes of town, just as their ancestors had done since the Middle Ages in response to every outburst of Vesuvius. Even as the priest led his parishioners in prayer, the mountain erupted more violently than before. The night sky was lit by white-hot rocks ejected out of the crater and by the glow of lava that lingered perilously atop the precipice south of town.

Few local residents other than the Capassos were preparing to flee until, early on the morning of Monday, March 20, Vesuvius erupted again. A massive new lava stream moved down the upper slope into the Atrio del Cavallo and swept over the precipice in a cataract of fire, moving relentlessly across the flat farmland toward the village a quarter mile away. The local priest ordered the image of San Gennaro interred in a wine shop in the center of town, while his parishioners rushed home to gather their possessions.

U.S. Army trucks provided by the Allied Control Commission rolled out from San Sebastiano all day, carrying its frightened citizens to protected villages. Crossing the narrow roads leading to Cercola, San Giorgio a Cremano and Pollena-Trocchia, they edged past refugees and bleating livestock. By nightfall almost everyone in San Sebastiano had fled; only a few stubborn villagers remained behind with a detachment of Allied troops and Italian carabinieri.

The lava moved in spasms toward San Sebastiano. Through the night red spires rose from Vesuvius as heated boulders broke from the main flow of lava and bounded across the valley, igniting fruit trees. Coughing on sulfur fumes, Allied soldiers moved through San Sebastiano that evening, battering open doors with rifle butts and forcibly evacuating a few older, feeble residents who were reluctant to leave their homes.

Michele Capasso and his sons had already transferred all their possessions to Pollena-Trocchia, but they now decided to salvage part of their home. Tearing it apart, they loaded windows, doors, and steel beams into their cart. While Michele pulled away the last load by hand, his sons removed the front door from its hinges.

The lava was now only one hundred feet upslope from town. Flowing through newly planted fields, the lava periodically encountered shallow wells dug by the farmers to collect rainwater. Two small boys who had escaped the surveillance of the Allied troops stood near an uncovered well as the edge of the lava poured into it. The water boiled instantly, discharging a violent explosion that blasted boulders into the air, killing the boys.

As more wells ignited, Raffaele and Vincenzo Capasso hoisted the front door of their home over their heads to protect them against flying rocks. The brothers scurried downslope and ran across the iron bridge to the neighboring village of Massa di Somma, then headed toward the safety of Pollena-Trocchia, the front door still raised above their heads as a primitive shield.

Shortly after midnight, Tuesday morning, March 21, a thirty-foot-deep river of lava made its first contact with San Sebastiano, reaching a high wall surrounding the courtyard of the house closest to Vesuvius. For a moment the wall seemed to withstand the massive flow; then it suddenly disintegrated as flames shot from one corner of the stone structure. One wall fell in, then the entire house split in half, disappearing beneath the molten rock, which moved on relentlessly toward the center of town.

During the next three hours, San Sebastiano was annihilated as lava churned its way along Via Roma, demolishing everything in its path. By 3:30 in the morning the flow reached the iron girder bridge where the Allied Control Commission had set up a command post. The lava carried off the bridge, incorporating the melted steel into its glowing body, and continued on into the neighboring village of Massa di Somma, surrounding, then crushing, the church.

By early morning, San Sebastiano was smoldering, its Via Roma covered with lava to a depth of forty feet. Most of its residents were homeless, and all that was left of the town was a black river of volcanic stone emitting stinking fumes.

Raffaele Capasso lit another cigarette, and in a subdued voice talked about the years since the 1944 eruption.

"Two-thirds of the houses were destroyed in San Sebastiano. Before, there were two thousand people; only three or four hundred were left. The only water available came from one public fountain in the town. There were no public lights. The whole town was under millions of meters of lava and it was impossible to recognize the streets and properties of the people."

San Sebastiano lay desolate for a decade. The older people, especially, were saddened; one sorrowful man killed himself. Determined to revitalize the village, the younger members of a committee formed to reconstruct the village were moved to action. There was talk of incorporating the remains of the town into the neighboring village of San Giorgio a Cremano, but the people of San Sebastiano preferred to rebuild under their own jurisdiction, as had their ancestors. As mayor, they chose young Raffaele Capasso, a Socialist who has held the post for twenty-five years while rebuilding the village into a modern showcase. "People move here from Naples, Portici and other towns because it is so nice," the mayor boasted.

Because of Capasso, trees must be planted first in modern San Sebastiano. Only then can the houses be built. The mayor is a self-congratulatory politician, yet his satisfaction seems justifiable. I stood on his elevated terrace and looked down the street, where sunlight and shade played upon a variegated view of emerald hues. The new San Sebastiano is an enclave of serenity that pretends to be oblivious of the volcano above it.

"Don't you worry that it might all happen again, that Vesuvius will once more destroy San Sebastiano?" I asked.

An involuntary movement of an eye was his only hint of unease. "People don't want to hear about a possible eruption of Vesuvius," he hedged. "They think it's bad luck to talk about it. We are going to have a kind of plant and flower show to educate the people to love green and not destroy it. But we hide ourselves in that show. Most of all we want to organize a defensive program against an eruption of Mount Vesuvius. So at the show there will be volcanologists, geologists and naturalists who will come and talk. We want to create a national park around Vesuvius."

Such a park, he explained, would halt the otherwise inevitable expansion of housing and farming up the slopes of Vesuvius. Capasso envisions the black stream of 1944 lava one day covered with freshly planted pine seedlings.

"Good," I acknowledged. "But what about the areas already built up? What about San Sebastiano? What could be done to stop lava from coming down upon the town again?"

"There's a big argument going on about what could be done," the mayor replied. "For example, bombs could be used to deviate the course of lava. But between saying things and doing things there's a big difference."

As I walked through town after leaving the mayor's house I was cheered by the sight of the daily activity of the residents. I circled through the side streets until I came upon a minuscule alley appropriately called Via Vesuvio, where ahead of me loomed a twenty-foot wall composed of tiers of coal-black lava jammed against the side of a small apartment building. Greenery pushed through in places, the beginnings of nature's reclamation. I walked up concrete steps set into the lava to discover a dirt path that twisted to the top of the black stream.

Clearing the crest, I found myself in the backyard of fifty-four-year-old Mario Iorio and his wife, Anna, who was planting flowers in three dirt-filled washtubs. She wiped her hands against her flaring orange apron as I approached, sidling nervously between me and the sight of her girdle, drying on the clothesline. Two mongrels at her feet barked at me.

Mario stepped outside to see the cause of the commotion. A frayed gray jacket was draped loosely over his shoulders, the arms swinging free. The Iorios were guarded at first, but they became talkative when I asked about Vesuvius. "All the buildings here," Mario said, gesturing with his left hand, "are built upon lava." He was raised on this spot, but his original house was now buried somewhere in the rubble upon which we stood. When a new house was built on the site, he moved back to San Sebastiano, because this is his home.

At the southern edge of town, near the place where two boys were killed by a water well explosion during the 1944 eruption, I rested upon a mound of lava and smoked my pipe. Across the road two men rattled jackhammers while a third shoveled pieces of lava out of a ditch. The black rock underlies this whole city block, hidden for the most part by fresh white apartment buildings.

Armando de Luca lives in the apartment complex with his wife and five children, whom he supports by hauling construction supplies in his small green tricycle truck, the kind known as an *api* ("bee") because of the manner in which it buzzes about town. They still call Armando "The American," a nickname he acquired as a boy during the 1944 eruption by toddling alongside the Allied troops as they worked to evacuate the villagers and later helped in the resettling.

I chatted with him as he sat in the cab of his *api*. His family was fortunate in 1944, he told me. The lava moved precariously close to their house, but narrowly bypassed it. "Ten days ago I went up to the volcano to look around," de Luca said.

"Did you see anything that scared you?" I asked.

His reply was a model of Italian machismo, providing one clue as to why virile men do not move their women and children to a safer environment. Said de Luca: "I'm not scared of anything."

Leaving the de Lucas, I drove along a back road that paralleled the lava flow, and was soon at the base of the Atrio del Cavallo just south of San Sebastiano. Mount Somma rose precipitously on my left, Vesuvius even higher on my right. Turning back, I could trace the path of the lava, a black river more than two hundred yards wide flowing into the midst of San Sebastiano. I was startled to see that farmers had cleared small plots within the lava and were cultivating grapes, beans and tomatoes in the degenerate residue of previous eruptions. The new lava must disintegrate over centuries before it provides the base for a rich soil.

A farmer had constructed a lane by steamrolling the lava. I walked across this pathway, which was similar in appearance to an open coal bed, its fragments ranging from fine black grit to boulders taller than I, the pitchy tones highlighted with specks of what looked like cold cigarette ash. Yellow dandelions challenged the black domination of the igneous rock.

At the far side of the lava flow I introduced myself to Raffale Manzo, a man in his early forties, who was working his one-hectare farm with his wife, Antoinetta. Clad in muddy jeans and a light tan sweatshirt, he led me to a slight rise where he showed me the abandoned stone house that he and his family fled in 1944. Deluged by boulders, the house had remained standing, but was no longer habitable.

Today Raffale lives in the village of Massa di Somma, which directly adjoins San Sebastiano, but he and Antoinetta still farm the family plot, having cleared away most of the lava. In the crowded countryside, land is precious, and their small plot provides the Manzos' only income. They cart their harvest by hand to village markets. "It's good land if it rains," Raffale acknowledged, "but we have no rivers or water here. We have to depend upon the rain."

The moisture had been adequate this season. Manzo proudly showed me peas and beans flourishing in neat rows, terraced to conform to the contours of the rich brown soil that is curiously shaded with an ebony hue.

The attitude of the people of San Sebastiano toward Vesuvius was summed up for me by Francisco Spina, who supports his wife and four children by farming a small plot of land near Raffale Manzo's. He was cultivating peas in a field carved out of the same lava stream. Spina stopped work as I approached and offered a smile.

He was fourteen in 1944, old enough to remember fleeing with his family from their home on the northern outskirts of San Sebastiano. Francisco still remembers the elation he felt when he returned after the eruption to find that the lava flow had halted just before his home.

I asked him if he was worried that Vesuvius might someday destroy his fields or his home.

"It can explode anytime," he assured me, "but what can we do? Nothing." He stared into the bright sky and shrugged. "There's always God."

4

INTO THE CRATER

By 6:45 IN THE MORNING the sky was already turquoise, un-blemished by clouds except for a single gray cloak grazing the summit of the volcano. Once again I was climbing up the sharp final slope of Vesuvius. Stretching beneath me was a dusty layer of powdered snow from an unseasonal storm the evening before. The flakes muffled the normal crunch of stone underfoot as I and four other men trod upward on the trail toward the rim.

We were here at dawn to prepare for a descent into the crater of Vesuvius. I had walked the slopes of the volcano and had visited one of its victims, the village of San Sebastiano. Now I was preparing to see the place where its awesome power orig-inated.

I had no idea that the simple inquiry I had made a few days before would have crystallized so rapidly into an expedition. I was no mountain climber, yet I was undertaking a task that, although not unprecedented, was foolhardy for a neophyte.

The improbable adventure began with my offhand remark to Dr. Luongo about descending into the crater. Luongo had given me the telephone number of the Alpine Club in Naples. When I called, I was invited to the club's regular weekly meet-ing the following Tuesday night at the old Anjou castle near the commercial docks of Naples, a short walk from my hotel. The director was pleased to hear of my interest in Vesuvius, and introduced me to Giovanni Giannini, who had led the expedition down into the crater the previous year.

"You have climbed before?" Giovanni asked.

"No."

Giovanni thought for a moment. "It can be dangerous. Are you afraid?"

"Yes."

He beamed. "Good. We'll go, because you will listen to us."

The next morning Giovanni and three other Alpine Club members picked me up at the Hotel Vesuvio at 5 A.M. Before I had time to consider the risk, I found myself shivering in the morning air, climbing to the top of Vesuvius.

Giovanni, twenty-three, an engineering student at the University of Naples, was our acknowledged leader. Compactly built, his skills had been honed by spelunking and climbing. The second man was Enzo Albertini, twenty-one, a full-time wine-and-liquor salesman, part-time architectural student, whose prematurely balding scalp was protected by a red stocking. Noting my discomfort at the cold, Enzo reached into his backpack and handed me a whiskey miniature, one of his samples.

Our backup men were Carlo Piciocchi, twenty-eight, a mechanical engineer from Naples, and Rudi Graffi, also twenty-eight, an engineering student from the village of Portici, both of whom were heavily bearded. Dressed warmer than the rest of us, they would remain on top, handling the ropes, while Giovanni, Enzo and I descended into the crater.

Carlo and Rudi strode on ahead bearing heavy cylindrical yellow backpacks and a sledgehammer. By the time Giovanni, Enzo and I reached the summit, Carlo and Rudi were already hammering a three-foot stake into the hard-packed ground about fifteen feet from the edge of the crater.

The crater was saturated with fog. I was worried that it would block the panoramic view, but Giovanni assured me it would lift once the sun warmed the air. Wary of my footing, I approached the brink carefully and looked down. We were at the same point from which I had first viewed the crater with Dr. Luongo. According to the map on the observatory wall it was 525 feet down to the bottom.

The first thirty-six-foot stretch was a sheer drop down the face of a rocky cliff, which we would negotiate by rope and ladder to reach a narrow outcropping of stone. From this ledge we would then carefully make our way down the forty-five-degree slope of loose pebbles that blanket the innards of the pit for the greater part of the descent. Gazing down upon the initial drop of thirty-six feet, I was convinced that it was a far greater distance than I had been told. The ledge below appeared to offer only a tenuous perch.

My apprehension deepened when Carlo fumbled inside a backpack and produced a rickety metal ladder, tightly coiled and only eight inches wide. The rungs, spaced about sixteen inches apart, were quarter-inch aluminum rods strung together with wire that appeared to be as uncertain as my nerve.

Giovanni addressed me in faltering English. "We . . . Enzo and me . . . go down with rope. You get down with this. . . . " he indicated the ladder. "Carlo, Rudi, they hold you with the rope."

Carlo fitted me into an awkward harness with red suspender straps that looped over my shoulders, beneath my arms, around my waist and under my crotch. I quickly discovered that mountain climbing plays havoc with genitalia. In the center of the harness, at navel level, was a metal clasp, to which Carlo clipped an aluminum handle. Enzo thrust a pair of blue-and-white-striped leggings at me, which slid over the tops of my boots to keep loose stones out. A hard hat completed my outfit.

Enzo descended first, sliding easily down a rope to the ledge below. Giovanni and I would overtake him later, for he would be slowed by the task of playing out a half-inch yellow guide rope that we would use in the climb back up.

Giovanni coaxed me over to the edge of the cliff. He lifted the ladder from the ground and taught me to grasp it, not by the rungs or the sides alone, but from behind, fingers curled over the rungs, thumbs looped around the sides. "And when you are tired . . . this," he said, showing me how to clip my harness to the ladder in order to rest suspended in air.

As Giovanni edged toward the rope, the cloud cover over Vesuvius dissipated and the sun rose above the eastern rim to illuminate the crater below. "I go now," Giovanni said. "And after me, you."

He had disappeared before I could respond, leaving me alone with Carlo and Rudi, neither of whom spoke English. There was no way to back out now. Carlo fastened the safety rope securely to my harness as Rudi sprawled upon the ground at the rim and braced his legs stoutly against a massive boulder ten feet from the edge. The yellow rope stretched from my belt around Rudi's back to one of the imbedded iron stakes. Rudi would play out the rope in accord with Carlo's direction.

Reflecting later upon this moment, I theorized that cognition had deserted me; perhaps this is one of the mind's most effective defenses. How else could a moderately rational human being clutch the flimsy ladder Carlo offered and move to the edge of the crater of Vesuvius? How else could I have knelt on the ground and crawled backward until I felt the toes of my boots drop over the sheer edge of a five-hundred-foot cliff?

"Piano," Carlo cautioned. "Slowly."

One foot slipped down the ladder searching anxiously for the next rung. Ordering myself to move in slow motion, resisting the impulse to peer down, I eased the top of my body over the brink of the historic volcano.

My knuckles ground against the outcropping of rock, but I barely noticed the lacerations as I concentrated on finding the rung with my foot. After the first five feet, the face of the cliff wall turned slightly inward. My hands no longer slammed against the rock, but now the ladder twirled me slowly about in a circular pattern.

Deliberately, I moved downward, Carlo and Rudi playing out the rope a foot at a time. I was halfway down to the ledge when my foot slid off one of the slippery aluminum rungs and I stretched to lower myself two steps at a time.

"Billy!" Giovanni bellowed up. "One at a time. Careful."

I glanced down and more cautiously sought a foothold, realizing that a misstep would invite instant death. I continued to descend the slowly rotating ladder until the toes of my boots touched the ledge below. I grinned at Giovanni perched just beneath me on a second platform of rock. At this point we encountered a painful communications breakdown. I stood tiptoe on the ledge, a prisoner of my taut safety rope, the harness cutting sharply into my groin. "I need more rope. I can't move," I called out.

Giovanni finally saw the predicament mirrored in my reddening face and called up at Carlo for more rope. The line slackened about an inch, but agony still engulfed me.

"More!" I cried.

Giovanni called again and the rope slackened sufficiently for me to unclip it from my harness. Now free from the lifeline, I stepped carefully down to where Giovanni stood upon a platform fashioned of several large boulders.

"Okay?" he asked.

"Okay." The pain subsided quickly, replaced by the joy of accomplishment.

I could not believe that I was inside Vesuvius, but the setting proved convincing. From this vantage point the crater seemed considerably more voluminous than when viewed from above. We were encased within a jagged oval made up of alternating layers of smooth brown ash and gray slag. On three sides the walls rose hundreds of feet straight up; the fourth side was our pathway. There was certainly no route in or out of the crater other than the way we had come.

Ahead of us, sloping forty-five degrees downward, stretched an eight-hundred-foot-long ramp of small loose rock accented with clusters of larger gray-white boulders. The rocks seemed predominantly rust in color, but a closer inspection revealed a spectrum of hues—yellow, black, brilliant orange, a delicate marble and innumerable shades of red.

We would travel the remaining distance downward without the protection of a safety rope; a miscalculation could be fatal. With Giovanni in the lead, we set off to join Enzo, who was now fifty feet below us, slowly uncoiling the yellow rope that would aid us in our return. Giovanni jumped down from the ledge into the lengthy patch of loose rubble, angling his feet perpendicular to the slope to brake his slide through the stone. A few of the larger pieces dislodged and bounced downward, gathering speed as they converged upon Enzo.

"*Pietra!* Rock!" Giovanni shouted. "Enzo! *Pietra, pietra!*" Enzo looked up in time to rush off safely to our right as rocks flew past him with shotlike echoes bouncing off the crater walls.

I followed Giovanni downslope in a series of sideways leaps, twisting in the air in order to land at a right angle to the incline. When we stopped for a moment, Giovanni flashed a disapproving eye at the brightening overhead sky, explaining that the greatest danger we faced was from falling rock. The crater constantly erodes in upon itself, a process accelerated by the warmth of the sun after a cold night. He would have preferred a cloudy day.

We followed the trail of loose stone downward until Giovanni pointed out dozens of large fumaroles, steam jets that had been invisible from the top. I wondered if the observatory volcanologists, none of whom have ever descended into the crater, were aware of the extent of this activity.

We labored over to the fumaroles. I thrust my hand into one and drew it back instantly, shaking off the pain.

"Hot!" Giovanni warned, too late.

The rocks surrounding the jets were pleasantly edged in velvet green moss. "Only here there is some vegetation," Giovanni said. "Because there is a fumarole. And also where there is ash, because ash is very fine."

Giovanni pointed to another steam vent near the face of the northern cliff. "We can't go there," he continued. "Just from the sound of voice comes rocks. *Pericoloso*—dangerous."

We rested until Enzo completed his task and joined us. Then, three abreast, with the two experienced climbers careful to keep me in the middle, we continued our journey downward.

My eye suddenly caught an unexpected sight. "Look!" I shouted. "Flowers." I had found a cluster sheltered behind a rock, delicate miniature white petals arranged symmetrically on dusty green stems, each group of blossoms no larger than my thumbnail. The fragile presence of these buds was out of character with their clime. "I'm going to take some home to my wife," I said, plucking a small sprig, placing it carefully in my lapel pocket.

We continued downward, now leaping more easily along the boulders until we came upon a series of large rock slabs that looked like a terraced staircase. We were nearing the bottom.

Enzo lingered for a moment atop one of the boulders. "Bill," he said, *"C'e un altro mondo."* I had to ponder that for a moment, translate. It's another world, he had said. If it were not for isolated bits of vegetation, we could have been marooned on a distant planet.

As the slope leveled off, Enzo and I walked toward one of

the great ash slides that sloped in from the sides of the cliffs. "Billy, stay in the middle," Giovanni warned. "Rocks can fall on you there."

Chastised, I followed him into the flattened circle, about fifty feet in diameter, that forms the crater base. Several sharp reports warned us that stones that had broken loose from the southern cliff were plummeting toward us, gaining speed. There was nowhere to run; we could only watch as the rock-slide neared the crater bottom, lost momentum and clattered to a stop thirty feet away. We all stood quietly for a time, and when we resumed speaking it was barely above a whisper. Giovanni told me that last year, an hour after he had left the crater, an earth tremor touched off boulder slides that surely would have proven fatal.

We continued downward until I was satisfied that we had reached the nadir of the volcano, a point at which a series of immense boulders formed a plateau. We sprawled upon them and surveyed our sovereign territory. I tilted my head back-ward and stared at the eastern edge, a stark cliff rising directly above us, incredulous at the thought that I was lying on my back at the very bottom of the crater of Vesuvius.

Enzo chattered something in Italian, which Giovanni trans-lated. "He said you are the only writer who ever came here." We remained at the bottom for more than an hour, gazing up at the tourists now arriving at the rim. It was impossible to dismiss the thought that should the volcano erupt at this mo-ment, we would be reduced to charcoal. The possibility seemed remote, yet was that not the rationale that had proved deadly for thousands of Campanians over the past two millen-nia?

I stared back up the slope, which suddenly seemed more formidable than ever. "Which is more difficult," I asked, "coming down or going up?"

"Going up," Giovanni answered candidly.

We began our return to the top of the crater, three abreast, at first easily scrambling up the gentle incline. But as the up-ward angle increased we encountered a stretch of loose slag in which my legs churned fiercely just to maintain a standing position. Most of the time I was reduced to crawling on my hands and knees, fearful of falling backward. My knuckles were soon scraped raw, my knees burning from ceaseless scuffing, my breath drained by the exertion.

My inexperience slowed the others considerably, but they were tolerant of me. Enzo moved ahead on the left by himself, for he would be the first to make the ascent. Our immediate goal was the point halfway up the slope where the yellow rope waited to assist us.

"You go now," Giovanni said. "I wait here until you finish."

I waded into the slag, slipped to my bruised knees, and slowly crawled over to the yellow lifeline a dozen feet to my left. Grasping the rope, I attached it to the handle that Carlo had clipped to my belt earlier. It seemed it would be a simple task to negotiate the next four hundred feet, but the surface was now nearly all loose stone and my legs churned aimlessly in the debris. Instead, I climbed with my arms, pulling my body upward inches at a time. My arms began to ache; my fingers grew numb.

I stopped to rest frequently, returning the encouraging waves of tourists who had gathered at the rim. Slowly, suffering intense pain, I pulled myself arm over arm toward Enzo, who waited at the base of the ladder.

I had now completed the first segment of my return, but the thought of the final climb of thirty-six feet straight up to the rim haunted me. My arms and legs were cruelly sore, in no condition for the climb. But I had no choice; somehow I had to negotiate this last obstacle.

Giovanni clipped the safety line to my harness as I positioned myself resolutely at the base of the ladder. I placed my left foot on the first rung as I kicked my right foot up toward the second rung. Determined to use my arms to lift myself up the ladder, I pulled heavily with my biceps. But a sudden pain coursed through my exhausted arms, causing me to uncurl my fingers.

Suddenly I fell loose from the ladder, hands and feet flailing, suspended above the crater only by the safety rope attached to my harness. Giovanni screamed out directions and in two excruciating jerks of the rope I was lowered back to the ledge below. I gasped for air.

"Billy," Giovanni counseled, "don't use arms, use . . . " He clutched his thighs. I now realized the mistake of my long climb up the yellow rope. I had pulled with my arms instead of pushing with my legs.

Looking up, I counted the rungs, a total of twenty between myself and safety. Concentrate on the first ten, I thought. This time I pushed off the ground, grasping the ladder with my arms only after my legs had first provided lift. I counted the rungs: "Three . . . four . . . five." I stopped momentarily, exhausted but determined not to relinquish the steps I had conquered. "Six . . . seven . . . eight." Then quickly, "Nine . . . ten." I had to rest. My fingers groped for the clip on my belt, which I snapped into place on the ladder.

"Billy!" Giovanni called up. "Good. Now you can just lay back for a minute." Kicking my feet off the rungs, I released my handhold. I was suspended in midair, held fast to the ladder by the clip. The strain on my crotch was worth the moment's respite for my arms and legs.

After a short rest, I returned to the ascent. Ten more rungs, I reminded myself, as I started to count in reverse. "Nine . . . eight." I would not pause now. I was beyond pain and fatigue. "Four . . . three," I cried out loud.

Carlo and Enzo peered at me over the precipice. There were only two rungs left, but I could not move. My contorted movements had twisted the safety line behind the ladder, where my weight had pinned it against the rocky outcropping. The only way to free the rope was to remove my weight from the ladder. The thought was terrifying.

I swung my legs off the ladder, at the same time pushing it to one side, freeing the rope. I dangled in the air, held above the chasm only by Rudi's strength. For traction, I gouged my knees into the vertical side of the cliff, then caught the rope with flailing hands. Somehow I pulled myself up the rope two feet closer to the top. Though neither was secured by a lifeline, Carlo and Enzo leaned out over the precipice, reaching down to me. Enzo clutched my right hand as Carlo grabbed my left. They pulled me quickly over the edge.

I staggered to my feet, drained of energy, exultant to be back on safe ground. Enzo propped me up in front of a boulder, and proffered a miniature whiskey. I wanted to express my gratitude, but I knew only the simplest Italian. *"Signore!"* I bellowed hoarsely. All four turned to look at me. *"Grazie!"*

They laughed. Giovanni said in Italian, "That sounded like the ultimate thank you."

5

THE FIRST VICTIM

I HAD SEEN THE INNARDS of Vesuvius. Now I felt compelled to see the volcano's first victim, Pompeii, the ancient city whose death on August 24, A.D. 79 had made the volcano notorious.

I was curious about that infamy. Was the destructive potency of Vesuvius exaggerated in the romantic novels that portrayed Pompeii's end? Or was the volcano's power a reality frozen into the ruins of this Roman city?

One Saturday morning I bought a ticket to Pompeii on the Circumvesuviana Railway that runs between Naples and Sorrento. The platform was crowded with passengers making their way to and from the villages that fill the Vesuvian landscape. We stopped at three stations on the outskirts of Naples, then made two stops each in San Giorgio a Cremano, Portici, and Ercolano. At Torre del Greco, Vesuvius could be seen directly out the window to my left, four miles off. On this morning four miles seemed like a safe distance; I had to remind myself that Pompeii is two miles farther away from the volcano.

After stops at Torre dell' Annunziata and Boscotrecase, we came to Boscoreale, once the king's hunting grounds, now dirty and poor. Vesuvius was behind us when the train stopped at the station designated *Pompei Scavi*—Pompeii Excavations. I stepped to the platform along with a young couple in blue jeans, knapsacks on their backs, and followed them to a brick guardhouse where I paid a 150-lire admission fee, about eighteen cents for a visit to Pompeii.

The couple walked on ahead. I purposely let them drift out of sight, for it seemed appropriate to be alone. It was shirtsleeve warm and there was no human sound, except for my muffled tread on the dirt path. The pathway led downward, then leveled and wound about to an ancient cobbled road, which was narrow and true, a testimony to Roman engineering. The pavement was composed of rounded inlaid blocks of smooth, light-gray stone, each two or three feet in diameter, with tufts of green pushing up at their junctures. The road was bounded by two-foot curbs of rectangular stone and led through an arched, ivy-covered gateway. Along either edge of the roadway was a deep rut, the unmistakable mark of decades of rumbling cart traffic.

Tourism is so often a wearying, programmed disappointment that I could scarcely believe my luck. I was in a prime tourist site on a Saturday and was alone. I walked past dozens of ruined hovels, each smaller than my hotel room, built with walls composed of stones the size of my fist and held together by mortar. In a few places the original veneer of thin brick was still evident. The ceilings, where they were intact, were uncomfortably low.

I ducked into one room and tried to imagine life in such a tiny cubicle. The house of the average Pompeiian family was wedged into a narrow street with a common wall shared with a neighbor. A single chafing dish over a fire often served as the kitchen, with a latrine hole nearby. Few of these humble homes were excavated beyond the walls that bordered the street, but here and there was a complete room, carpeted now with weeds, traces of faded yellow or rose-colored pigment still visible upon the interior walls.

The first complete house appeared on my left, a placard on the lintel proclaiming it to be the home of M. Obelli Firmi. Entrance was barred by a green gate, through which I could see a cracked marble slab leading to an atrium guarded by four pillars. The compluvium above, the hole for collecting rainwater, was clogged with moss and weeds.

I moved farther into the city, still heading westward. A bright green lizard raced ahead of me across the threshold of a ruin. Inside I found a red stucco wall decorated with geometric lines, crumbling into pieces. A red and white shrine, resembling a child's drawing of a house, was recessed into one of the walls.

Close by, a shop, or perhaps a bar with an L-shaped marble countertop hollowed out to hold clay wine casks called amphorae, opened into the street. Next door, unmistakably, was a bakery with three stone mills and a brick hearth resembling a present-day Neapolitan pizzeria oven.

At the intersection of a side street to my right, the now-familiar four-thousand-foot western cone of Vesuvius soared over Pompeii in quiet dominance. The horizon that Pompeiians viewed in A.D. 79 was even more impressive: a single peak of far greater circumference that stretched half again as high as the present Vesuvius.

I seemed to be moving into a more affluent section of large homes that were unquestionably lavish in their day. I stopped to examine one of them, the House of the Faun, which exhibited the opulence of Pompeii of legend. The entrance led across an inlaid mosaic threshold of white, orange, blue and violet plaster tiles through to a roofless atrium. In the midst of the impluvium, the pool for collecting rainwater, stood the delicate bronze statue of a dancing faun, his arms joyously uplifted, thanking the gods for the bounty of rain that poured in on his head. Faded pink and yellow wall panels hinted at a bright interior decor.

Off the atrium were small, dark bedrooms, their size typical of even the grander homes. Beyond was a massive courtyard, now filled with crumbling columns, shrubs and weeds. The residents of this town mansion must have felt impenetrably secure, but today their home is a museum piece in a ruined city.

I soon found a tourist restaurant, a modern brick-and-glass structure, incongruous in the ancient surroundings. At the gift shop I bought an English guidebook and settled down with a cup of coffee. The maps showed a rough oval of a town, about three-quarters of a mile in diameter at its widest point. I had entered from the most remote part of the city, which accounted for my isolation. The main gate was on the opposite side near the Villa of the Mysteries station of the Circumvesuviana line. I could see that nearly 75 percent of Pompeii has been excavated, and most of the remaining sites were in the humble residential quarter I had first seen.

To answer my questions about the current state of the ruins,

I searched out Stefan de Caro, chief of the Bureau of Excavations at Pompeii, whose office was located in the shell of an ancient home on Via Consolare, not far from the restaurant. He was a genial man in his early thirties, with a bushy black moustache plastered above his grin.

"We have no plans to excavate the rest of Pompeii," he explained. "There is too much to do with the excavated portions, to restore and preserve them." This restoration had been under way for several years when the 1980 earthquake damaged hundreds of Pompeii's ancient structures. De Caro was forced to close the ruins to the public for a time until his workers could strengthen both the weakened buildings and famed columns that surround the open Forum.

De Caro asked an assistant, Alfredo, a friendly man of slight build in his late fifties, to show me several exhibits normally closed to casual visitors. Alfredo led me east from de Caro's office to a small side street to the Vicolo dei Vettii. Pompeii abounds with wealthy town mansions that reflect the decadence of that society, and the House of the Vettii brothers on the street that bears their name is one of the best-preserved examples of that Pompeiian indulgence.

Alfredo unlocked the barred doors and showed me ancient graffiti scratched into the stone above the threshold. From this, and from two inscribed bronze rings found inside, we know that the house belonged to the brothers Aulus Vettius Restitutus and Aulus Vettius Conviva, "two bachelors who lived together and did commerce," as Alfredo explained.

He turned to the right of the vestibule and pointed to a small wall painting depicting the god Priapus leaning against a pillar. His left hand had drawn his tunic above his waist to reveal an enormous erect penis reaching down nearly to his knee. The penis rested upon a scale. "It's worth its weight in gold," Alfredo laughed.

Phallic symbols were commonly found throughout Pompeii, but they were less shocking in that culture than in ours. The penis was a symbol of birth, and birth an omen of prosperity. In many shops a representation of an erect penis was used as a bellpull to announce the arrival of a customer. One can assume, however, that the omnipresent image was also used to promote hearty ribaldry, as a further examination of the House of the Vettii indicated.

The entranceway opened onto an expansive atrium, one of the largest in all Pompeii, decorated with murals of bright, hovering cupids. The house was a duplex in which each brother maintained his own sleeping quarters and offices on opposite sides of the building, but shared the lavish common rooms in between. On either side of the entrance room was a weighty iron money chest, one for each brother. Each brother also kept his own watchman installed in a cubicle near the door, an indication that commercial interests may have outweighed filial ties.

Beyond the atrium the house opened into a peristyle now outfitted with local archaeological finds to simulate a Pompeiian garden of the day. Water spurted through lead pipes into decorative birdbaths and fountains. At one end of the rectangular court, two bronze boys squirted water into a basin carved from rare translucent alabaster. Not on exhibit, but discovered here, was a fountain-statue of a lecherous man gushing water from his own penis.

Alfredo drew me off to the triclinium, the dining room where the host and his guests reclined upon the three attached couches, a unit patterned after the Greek letter π. The open end allowed access by servants. Slaves sliced the food before serving it on silver dishes to the diners, who ate with spoons while lounging on their left elbows. Main courses of fish, chicken, oysters, pork, or even venison roasted in cultured honey were served with abundant vegetables and fruits and great draughts of wine.

As the Vettii brothers gorged themselves, they could admire a series of small wall paintings that depicted miniature cupids engaged in a variety of occupations: making perfume, fashioning gold jewelry, laundering togas, baking bread, preparing and selling wine. Perhaps these enterprises were the businesses of the prosperous family. Many of the figures represented were portrayed with angelic wings, one of which surprisingly resembled Mary Poppins, attired like a nanny, flying out the doorway beneath an open parasol.

Alfredo's voice took on a conspiratorial tone as he beckoned me to follow him. As we approached a heavy steel door, he fingered a special key in his hand. Glancing around to ensure that no tourists were about, he unlocked the door and we entered a small dark room whose only source of light was narrow slit windows.

The wall was covered with erotic paintings. "The rich had rooms like this," Alfredo whispered, "where they took their foreign girls . . . slaves."

One crude painting detailed a naked woman sitting astride a reclining man. "That is the Pompeiian way," Alfredo proclaimed. A second painting showed a man sitting atop a woman, who had her left leg draped over his shoulder. "That," Alfredo announced, "is the Spanish way."

Alfredo led me out of the House of the Vettii to a building on Via dei Teatri several blocks south. Inside the house were many small cubicles opening off the short, dark central hallway. High on the corridor wall was another series of erotic paintings. The place was an ancient brothel, called *lupinare.* The term was derived from the Latin "lupa," or "she-wolf," a common Roman phrase for prostitute. Alfredo offered a fanciful explanation of the derivation of the word. Since many imported slave-prostitutes could not speak Latin, the madam had them lean out the window and howl like wolves toward the travelers lodged at the Inn of Sittius across the street.

Cash was not always necessary for these transactions, for the prostitutes kept accounts of the customers' debts scratched upon the wall, marks that are still visible today. The small faded frescoes high on the walls depicted nude couples in various positions of sexual intercourse, allowing the customer to indicate his preference.

Next door to the lupinare Alfredo showed me a pharmacy whose proprietor had once offered potions to ward off diseases that might have been contracted at the brothel. Farther along Strada dell' Abbondanza he pointed out a second, more sedate, brothel advertised by the inscription of an erect penis carved into the pavement, pointing toward the door of the establishment. Here, according to Alfredo, the prostitutes uncovered everything but their faces, because some of them were otherwise respectable matrons earning extra income.

The liberal sexual attitudes of Pompeii were like those of

any other seaport, ancient or modern. Pompeiian entrepre-
neurs were ready to fulfill the desires of visitors who came
from the ends of the Roman Empire to do business in the city.
Alfredo wondered how many local prostitutes were engaged
with their customers when Vesuvius erupted.

Most people think Pompeii is a static museum piece, an
entire city from brothels to mansions that has now been totally excavated. On the contrary, nearly half of the 450 employees at Pompeii are actively engaged in preserving
buildings discovered but not fully restored.

When I asked Alfredo to take me to one of these projects, he
led me to the western edge of Pompeii, to a large hotel constructed partly within the city wall, between the side streets
of Via di Termi and Vico dei Soprastanti. The building is now
called the House of Fabio Rufo, for his seal was found here.
But as excavation and restoration work proceeded, it became
obvious from the maze of subterranean sleeping cubicles that
this was actually a hotel, a fashionable overnight stop for seaside travelers.

Alfredo and I stepped through a wrought-iron gate into the
largest atrium I had seen in Pompeii. Urging caution, he ush-
ered me down a disintegrating stone staircase. We descended
into a dank basement, but after circling through a series of
halls, we emerged onto a pleasant portico whose large windows let in the sun.

Off this passageway was a series of bedrooms, decorated
with small mythological paintings set into black backgrounds.
In some rooms was fresh evidence of Vesuvian power: skeletons or plaster body casts entombed in protective glass cases.
At the base of a second stairway lay the body cast of a man,
his head resting upon the second step, his left arm extended,
his lifeless plaster eyeballs gazing upward toward the horror
descending upon him.

When the hotel is ready for public display in about five
years, it will become a prime Pompeiian attraction. Its underground rooms extend through nearly an entire city block, and
one is struck by the realization that so many of the patrons
never checked out of this hotel; instead they died in the eruption of August 24, A.D. 79. The excavators frequently find

bodies of unfortunate visitors who chose the wrong time to come to Pompeii and who, in the confusion of that day, made the fatal decision to remain inside their rooms.

In one cubicle off the lower-level peristyle on the south side of the hotel are two body casts that offer particularly vivid views of the moment of death. One man is turned onto his right side, curled in an instinctive reaction to the pain in his lungs. As the body cast shows, the man found next to him died in a push-up position, trying desperately to remove the weight of the rubble from his back.

As my guide motioned for me to follow him further, we retraced our route upstairs, carefully stepping over mosaic wall panels that workers were piecing together, finally arriving at a solid wooden door. As he searched for the key Alfredo confided, "These were found downstairs also. You will be the first visitor to Pompeii to see them."

The door swung open into a windowless room. I could see nothing until my companion flashed a light upon the plaster body casts of a family of four. The father lay upon his back, his head and left arm raised up in a terminal spasm. Nearby was the body of a three-year-old child, resting slightly on his left side, his arms curled above him, the folds of his tunic perfectly preserved in the plaster. His garment had worked its way above his waist, revealing him to be a boy.

Completing the grisly family portrait was a double image of two bodies in one cast. The mother was on her back, fists clenched in impotent fury. Welded to her in death was a baby, standing facing his mother, his feet placed securely on her stomach.

I wondered if this family of victims had any understanding of what had overtaken them. Did they look toward Vesuvius as the source of their agony? Did they have a scheme of faith to sustain them, or did they merely curse their useless gods and die?

Immediately south of the restaurant and gift shop is the high stone Arch of Caligula, leading to the Forum of Pompeii. I stepped through it into a wide grassy plaza that was as busy this day as it must have been two thousand years ago. Children now played among the stone columns, just as Pompeiian children had. This was the village square, the center of commerce and social life, with many important town buildings fronting upon it. Turning, I was treated to the classic view of Vesuvius, rising authoritatively above the remains of a proud culture.

The Temple of Jupiter stands guard at the north side of the Forum. As a warrior god, Jupiter was endowed with the capacity to summarily execute humanity with fiery thunderbolts forged for him by Vulcan, the god of subterranean fire. Today, Jupiter's shrine is only a cluster of abbreviated pillars, its brick façade gone, revealing the brown stonework beneath. Grass grows between wide steps that lead to a nonexistent altar.

The Roman religion was a pragmatic one in which there was no concept of divine affection and no concern with an afterlife. But by the second half of the first century A.D., there was a growing desire to move away from these quasi-human Greco-Roman gods toward mystical ideologies that offered hope, both in the present and in the future. The old gods were not totally forsaken, but new exotic deities soon became venerated.

Pompeii was a cosmopolitan seaport where foreign sailors and imported slaves brought their own gods to worship. From Egypt came the supreme goddess Isis, whose cult flourished despite the Roman Senate's castigation, a rebuke that lasted until Emperor Caligula established the goddess's legitimacy in A.D. 38. But by then she was already the most widely worshiped deity in the Roman Empire, and her temple in Pompeii was 150 years old.

The Temple of Isis—which was almost completely destroyed in the earthquake of A.D. 62 and subsequently reconstructed—centers upon a square shrine a short distance southeast of the Forum. It is divided into an open-air portico and a sacred back room closed off to the uninitiated. It has been documented that when the eruption began the priests were resting in the temple between the morning and afternoon services: Remnants of their lunch were found in the living quarters.

Ninety percent of what one sees at Pompeii is contained within the ancient city walls, but outside these walls, and still a part of Pompeii, are several lavish Roman villas. I followed Via dei Tombe north past the misnamed Villa of Cicero, past scores of ancient mausoleums, to the Villa of Diomed where several government employees had parked their motor scooters.

The wine merchant who owned this home obviously lived a luxurious life. The villa was built on two levels, but it was in the rear, lower portion that the owner must have relaxed. Its rectangular walls enclosed a spacious garden surrounded by terraces, with a decorative fishpond in its center.

The Villa of Diomed was one of the early sensational finds, excavated during the years 1771 to 1774. The diggers of those days, who were treasure hunters rather than archaeologists, ripped priceless mosaics off the walls and carted away numerous classical statues. One day their spades cut into the wine cellar under the north side of the garden.

I stood in that long, humid corridor and tried to imagine what the excavators had seen. Eighteen skeletons were entombed here with only a few small windows to allow in a portion of sunlight. One of these skeletons has continuously stimulated interest. It was that of a young woman, the bones of her hand clutching at her gold jewelry.

The excavation occurred before the invention of the body cast technique, but a whim of nature has left an impression of this woman that has inspired poets and novelists to ecstasy. She had pulled her fine gauzy tunic over her head in a futile attempt to ward off death. As she did, she pitched forward to the soft earth, which has preserved a perfect mold of one of her ample breasts.

There is much at Pompeii that causes one to shudder, but this room was one of the worst. Its damp, claustrophobic environment made me feel as though the walls were pressing in. I headed up the stone stairs and out to the garden, past the fishpond, up marble slab steps to the back iron gate where the bodies of the wine merchant and his slave were found attempting to escape from Vesuvius almost two thousand years ago.

Further down Via dei Tombe I passed through a narrow gate where a sign warned me to keep my admission ticket if I planned to reenter the city. I walked the few hundred feet to the Villa of the Mysteries, a lavish suburban home renowned for its nearly life-size series of frescoes depicting the initiation of a young woman into the mysteries of the cult of Dionysus, the god of pleasure. The wall panels in the Villa of the Mysteries portray various Dionysiac rituals, including a woman suckling a young goat, the unveiling of a huge phallic symbol, flagellation and nude dancing. In the mural, the initiate seems to change by stages from an innocent girl to a knowing woman.

The frescoes survived the eruption of A.D. 79 and subsequent threats from Vesuvius, but in late November 1980 the earthquake that killed three thousand people in southern Italy shook the Villa of the Mysteries and cracked one of these famed panels. For a time the villa was closed to the public.

I circled through the building, pausing in a basement cubicle to view the body cast of a screaming man, doubled over in pain. The damp gloom of the room accented the ghostly image of the soiled gray plaster of Paris that contained his ancient bones. On that August day, he had obviously felt, or seen, the horror of Vesuvius violently encroaching upon Pompeii.

Back outside the villa, I glanced toward the north. Here, as everywhere around Pompeii, Vesuvius is the giant. I thought of the screaming man in the basement. What had he known about Vesuvius other than what the Greco-Roman superstitions had told him? He was obviously unaware of the explosive potential of the earth on which he walked.

6

THE MECHANICS OF DEATH

THE DEATH CASTS at Pompeii haunted me, their mouths agape, screaming a silent question across the centuries: "How did we die?" These ghostly white forms had once been human, then in a single moment confusion and blackness engulfed them as the volcano struck. Nineteen hundred years later their flesh has turned to chalky white Plaster of Paris, their humanity replaced by a frozen gasp.

How do volcanoes kill? What are the mechanics of death that take place during a volcanic eruption? It was my challenge to answer these questions, and in doing so, discover how Vesuvius killed the Pompeiians. I added one more relevant query: Was Vesuvius capable of another explosion similar to the cataclysm of A.D. 79?

Paolo Gasparini, professor of geophysics at the University of Naples, who doubles as director of the Vesuvian Observatory, is considered an authoritative source on recent research into volcanic mechanisms. From my hotel it was a confusing ride through clogged streets to the university, a collection of unrelated stone structures wedged into the decaying central city. To find Gasparini's office I had to traverse a maze of hallways decorated with political graffiti.

After a half-hour search I located Gasparini, a diminutive, energetic man who explained to me that his primary mission is neither research nor classroom instruction. Instead, he feels compelled to educate the millions who live within Vesuvius' range to acknowledge the volcanic risk.

"The people around Naples think of Vesuvius as a dead volcano and that is dangerous," he commented. "The short repose periods are only due to the collapse of the crater upon the vent and nothing else. Practically speaking, the activity has been continuous since 1631. The magma has always been close to the surface."

Gasparini and his colleagues are frustrated. They are unable to penetrate the Neapolitan apathy in spite of a quantum leap in scientific understanding of volcanic mechanisms. Within the world geologic community there was resurgence of interest in volcanoes well before Mount St. Helens gave the subject frightening immediacy. Geologists have now developed new theories that contradict old explanations, and have even gained the ability to predict roughly when some volcanoes will erupt.

Over espresso we discussed this geological revolution, particularly the new information on the ways a volcano kills. Gasparini explained that volcanoes are versatile, producing a variety of agents that can be fatal to humans: lava, pyroclastic flows, ash, mud slides, poisonous gas and acid droplets, along with such fatal byproducts as lightning.

In order for Vesuvius to erupt, it must first clear a passage that has been blocked by erosion and ground collapse. This usually requires an earthquake, or at least earth shocks sufficiently powerful to dislodge the material choking the opening. Once the eruption begins, "bombs," or boulders weighing many tons, are hurled for miles in every direction.

Mankind is more familiar with the smaller products of an eruption, particularly the ash that covers homes, roads and countryside, which has long been postulated as the killer of Pompeii. The word "ash" is an unfortunate geological term, for it conjures a vision of light, airy particles wafting from the sky. On the contrary, volcanic ash is a viscous wet paste of small particles that may be driven almost horizontally by hurricane-force winds generated by pulsating explosions from the erupting crater. A particularly copious ash fall can suffocate its victims, but more often death results when ash accumulates and overloads the rooftops of buildings, causing them to collapse.

The intense eruption of the volcano breaks the subterranean material into other fine particles including small stones called lapilli, which range from the barely visible to golf ball size.

They are ejected from the underground chamber of molten rock and fall down at the whim of the prevailing air currents. Another fine particle, called pumice, is so saturated with gas that it floats upon water. When quantities of pumice shower a target area they can release volumes of lethal gas.

Lava is the agent popularly associated with volcanic eruptions. It has been a great destroyer of property, having razed dozens of towns in Campania, but these hot effusions generally move too slowly to endanger life. A lesser-known mechanism, pyroclastic flow, has more often been the lethal agent of an erupting volcano.

"A pyroclastic flow is much more dangerous than lava," the professor declared. Gesturing with his hands, Gasparini demonstrated how a sudden volcanic explosion can shoot a column of molten magma upward, causing it to crash back to the upper slopes and send a flood of gas-saturated superheated rock down the mountainside. "Anyone unlucky enough to be caught in the path of a pyroclastic flow will be killed," he declared simply. "You cannot escape."

Volcanologists first became aware of pyroclastic flows in 1902, when Mt. Pelee on the Caribbean island of Martinique hurled a burning avalanche down on the town of St. Pierre. Within minutes, 29,933 people died. Only four survived.

Normally, innocent mud is also transformed into a fatal substance by volcanic action. Airborne ash, combining with the enormous quantities of water vapor liberated by an eruption, creates an electrically charged atmosphere that produces forked lightning and violent rains. These tempestuous thunderstorms may last for days after the culmination of an eruption. Beating upon the fresh volcanic debris and accumulated ash deposits remaining from previous eruptions, the rain creates "lahars," or mud slides, which race downslope at speeds approaching thirty miles an hour, a momentum sufficient to carry well into the footlands. "It was such a lahar that buried Herculaneum," Gasparini said.

An ash explosion frequently generates another killing force, a cloud of invisible poisonous gas. It is gas, in fact, that is the primary driver of an explosive volcano. Here, Gasparini backed up in his discourse to explain the origin of the gas in subterranean reservoirs. Drawing on the theory of "plate tectonics,"

Gasparini and his colleagues in geology have considerably expanded their knowledge about the mechanisms of volcanoes, including how an eruption actually starts.

Plate tectonics is a theory that views the surface of the earth, including the ocean floor, as composed of huge "plates" in perpetual motion relative to one another. The edges of the plates, where land masses collide, form the world's major fault line systems and the locations of most earthquakes and volcanoes. At certain boundaries one plate slides over its neighbor, forcing the lower plate back into the earth's mantle. Here, the internal heat of the earth melts the old crust, creating a magma chamber—a solution of hot liquid rock—and liberates gases consisting of carbon dioxide and sulfur dioxide. Such magma chambers seem to underlie the entire western coast of Italy.

The accumulating gases may build sufficient pressure and burst upward through the crust, particularly where the surface has been weakened by faults, creating a volcanic eruption. The most violent explosions, however, are now believed to be fired by a third gas, which is not the product of the magma melt, but is derived from ground water, or "juvenile water," the primordial moisture of creation that has never reached the earth's surface.

Due to processes not fully understood, water at times comes into contact with a magma chamber. The suddenly heated water changes into its gaseous form, steam. It instantly expands a thousandfold and rises rapidly, carrying magma, its gases, and the adjacent debris with it. Once in the atmosphere, the gases become involved in lethal chemical reactions. Carbon dioxide dissolves into water vapor to form carbonic acid. Sulfur dioxide combines with water vapor to form deadly sulfuric acid, which may be synonymous with the Biblical term "brimstone." Droplets of such invisible acid can kill with a single breath.

"It is usual for a volcano to exhibit one, two, possibly three of these various mechanisms," Gasparini said. "Some volcanoes, like the Hawaiian ones, generally only effuse lava. Some always vent great ash explosions, others mainly pyroclastic flows. Vesuvius is one of the few volcanoes known to have done all these things frequently."

I then ventured a statement based on all I had learned about the great eruption of A.D. 79. "I understand that it was an ash explosion, with associated gas, that killed the people of Pompeii."

This was the commonly held view, Gasparini agreed, but recent studies at Vesuvius have convinced him that this traditional theory is false. There is, he emphasized, a new explanation for the death at Pompeii, one that has been accepted by all the Vesuvian volcanologists. This newly defined mechanism is known as a "base surge," a force that mimics the shock wave of a nuclear explosion. Gasparini suggested that his colleague Lucio Lirer, professor of mineralology, would be the best person to explain the base surge to me. I found him at his office at the university and what he told me would completely alter my conception of the lethal power of Vesuvius, and that of other volcanoes as well.

In 1973, Lucio Lirer was studying the ancient layers of pumice stone at Pompeii. While sifting through the upper layer of what he thought to be volcanic ash, he discovered large stone fragments too heavy to be the products of an ash explosion. He speculated that these stones did not fall vertically from the sky but exploded horizontally across the open countryside from the volcano. Together with Franco Barberi of the University of Pisa, he has since studied the possibility that this horizontal action was the true killing mechanism in the eruption of A.D. 79.

The traditional theory that the deaths at Pompeii were caused by a severe fallout of ash and the associated effects of poisonous gas and acid is based upon two facts. First: Most of the bodies were found on top of the initial six-foot layer of pumice and at the base of the second layer of material, thought to be ash, indicating immediate fatalities at the onset of this eruptive phase. Second: The body casts of the victims clearly depict a painful, choking death due to a combination of asphyxiation and poisoning. Scores of volcanologists expressed their doubt that an ash explosion could cause such an immediate catastrophe, but in the absence of other evidence it seemed the only reasonable explanation.

The information gained from a 1946 United States detonation of a twenty-kiloton underground nuclear device at Bikini atoll suggested a different geological scenario at Pompeii. Physicists observed the expected mushroom cloud rising vertically from the test site, but they did not anticipate the debris that surged horizontally along the ground at more than 130 miles per hour.

The same phenomenon was documented during the 1965 eruption of the Taal volcano in the Philippine Islands. Geologist James G. Moore noted that ". . . series of debris-laden eruption clouds moved out radially from the base of the main explosion column. These clouds carried blocks, lapilli, and ash suspended in water vapor and gases and moved outward with tremendous velocity. They shattered and obliterated all trees within one kilometer of the explosion center. . . ."

"A base surge travels very fast over the ground, perhaps sixty miles an hour, so that it just destroys everything that it finds," Lirer explained. "If it strikes a house, the walls standing parallel to the flow will stay up. The other walls will go down. It destroys whatever it finds perpendicular to the flow."

"How do we know that this is really what happened at Pompeii?" I asked.

"You can see it," he responded, sketching a diagram of volcanic strata. The drawing showed that near the vent of the volcano a base surge produces cross-lamination, long linear waves that resemble sand dunes. No other volcanic action creates this characteristic wavelike structure.

"You can see this in the strata at some of the excavations close to Vesuvius," Lirer said. "But Pompeii is too far away. As you go farther away from the volcano the structure of the base surge changes completely. Its energy is less. It thins out and it doesn't have the power to make a wave structure."

The evidence for the base surge at Pompeii is more subtle than cross-lamination, but no less conclusive. According to Lirer, when volcanic ash explodes into the air it is carried off by the prevailing winds, while the heavier particles fall to the ground. In a base surge the opposite occurs: The larger particles are carried along the ground farther from the vent than the smaller debris. Lirer's microscopic examination of the "ash" layer shows clearly that, at Pompeii, the farther one travels from Vesuvius, the larger the particles grow, striking evidence that the destruction occurred as a result of a horizontal base surge similar to the action witnessed at Bikini atoll, and not from ash falling from the sky.

Lirer explained that a base surge is consistent with the manner in which the Pompeiians died. The particulate matter swept along the ground by a base surge is thought to be cooler than that of a pyroclastic flow, or lava, but still quite hot. At Pompeii it may have been hot enough to sear the lung tissues of its victims, or so dust-laden that it choked them. Lethal quantities of sulfuric acid vapor also may have been fatal agents. Like a nuclear shock wave, the base surge would have thrown the victims to the ground, where they would have succumbed to the combination of heat, dust and gas descending from the mountain.

The immediate cause of death was this same combination, but the killing agents were delivered in a manner quite different from that which was previously supposed. Instead of showering down from the sky over a period of hours, they were sent across the ground in one immediate, deadly surge.

Prior to Lirer's work, the observatory volcanologists prepared two scenarios to help understand what could happen to the countryside during the next eruption of Vesuvius. The first possibility is a lava flow from the center of the crater, similar to the eruption of 1944, which would probably destroy San Sebastiano once again as well as other villages in the area.

The second possibility is an explosion from vents on the sides of the mountain slopes along fault lines that intersect directly beneath the crater. The most probable location of such new vents is along the western slope. In this scenario, the town most likely to suffer would be Torre del Greco on the bay west of Vesuvius, a frequent victim of the volcano.

Now a third, more alarming, scenario has been raised by the base surge theory, explained to me by Dr. Giuseppe Luongo on a return visit to the Vesuvian Observatory.

"We realize that we have a new threat," he explained. "We have to increase the level of risk for the whole area."

"Because of a possible base surge?"

"Yes."

"What are the areas that are more at risk from a base surge?" I asked.

"Everywhere."

"Even Naples?"

"Yes," he answered resignedly.

A base surge travels with such force that natural obstacles are easily overcome, Luongo explained. He gestured with his hands to mimic a flood of molten rock exploding laterally out of Vesuvius and rushing over the ridge of Mount Somma toward those villages that have always felt protected by the old volcanic shell.

I wanted to see, firsthand, evidence that would corroborate the theory that a base surge had been the mechanism of death in the eruption of A.D. 79. During my journey around Campania, I had heard of an excavation at Boscoreale dating back to the first century A.D. Since it was closer to Vesuvius than Pompeii itself, I wondered if it would show the peculiar cross-lamination markings produced by a base surge. I engaged a driver-interpreter, Angela Lauro, and set out one morning to find the ancient villa.

Boscoreale (literally "royal woods," for the Bourbon kings hunted there) is on a direct line between Vesuvius and Pompeii, four miles south of the volcano and two miles north of the ruins. There was no town of Boscoreale in A.D. 79, but there were a few isolated farming villas that were obliterated.

Boscoreale is nothing like the larger seaside towns of Torre del Greco and Torre dell' Annunziata. Being inland, it does not benefit from the commerce of the bay. Boscoreale's only activity is farming, and most of the plots are small and crowded. It is easy to understand why, each time Vesuvius lapses into repose, farmers extend their fields farther up the fertile slopes.

We found ourselves at a crossroad where stone walls surrounded olive and apricot groves. Angela stopped several passing cars and asked directions to the excavations, but no one seemed to have heard of the villa. Finally, a burly man on a motorcycle told us it was near a church.

Several wrong turns later we found the excavations hidden behind an apartment building. I was surprised to see a busy work crew, for the villa at Boscoreale was a nineteenth-century find and the excavation should have been completed long ago. We walked through a gate toward a small workmen's shack, where below us, to the right, the villa lay in a square pit covered over by a screen.

A man stepped from the shack and announced that the site was not open to the public. Angela rapidly changed his attitude by introducing me with the magical title "professore." Vincenzo Matrone smiled and shook my hand. He was a jovial man in his early forties who had been employed at Pompeii and only recently was placed in charge of this site. I asked if I could see the villa and the bodies that I understood had been found here.

"We have found no bodies here," Matrone said, perplexed.

An extended discussion in Italian clarified the matter. The villa I had read about had been covered over after the excavators removed its treasure, its location lost. This villa had been found only recently, which explained Matrone's surprise at our visit. Only a few archaeologists at Pompeii knew of its existence.

"Have any of the volcanologists from the observatory been here?" I asked.

"No," he told me.

Matrone led us down a sloping dirt ramp about twenty feet below to the remains of a rather ordinary wine-producing farm of the first century A.D. It had been discovered when builders sank concrete pillars for an addition to the nearby apartment complex. By Italian law such discoveries must be reported to government authorities, and this fresh excavation was the result.

We reached the bottom of the slope and turned at a right angle, facing the eastern wall of the seventy-five-foot-square pit. I stopped in amazement. Here, unknown to any of the Vesuvian volcanologists, was a perfect confirmation of Lirer's theory. The eastern and western walls pointed directly to Vesuvius, four miles to the north. The careful dig revealed a clear six-foot deposit of pumice, on top of which was a somewhat thicker layer of fine brown dirt that Matrone called volcanic ash. There were perhaps five or six feet between the upper and lower portions of the wave cycle, but ash does not fall this way. This was cross-lamination, the signature of a base surge. No other volcanic action could have produced it.

As I climbed back up to the present ground level and stared

at Vesuvius, I realized that I had stumbled on additional proof that the volcano had killed with a mechanism as awesome as a nuclear bomb. It was an image that would remain with me every time I saw the mountain.

7

HERCULANEUM

THE DESTRUCTION OF POMPEII by a base surge, cascading bombs, ash, pumice and deadly acids and gases fulfills our image of the power of a volcano. The ancient city of Herculaneum died in a more unorthodox way, deluged by a massive "lahar," a mud slide of Vesuvian dirt and soil that traveled sharply downslope in an uninterrupted flow and buried the city.

This agent of death was also responsible for the town's extraordinary state of preservation. For two millennia the dried mud has maintained the ancient ruins more effectively than did the base surge material at Pompeii.

From the train station at Ercolano in the town of Resina, I found my way along the humming Corso Resina to a wide concrete ramp that curved gradually downward to a point sixty feet below the surface, where ancient Herculaneum materialized before me. The town was lined with palm trees and comprised mainly of gray-walled blocks of houses, roofless to the sun, that almost gave the appearance of new construction. The whole of the excavated city, a square of seven-hundred-foot sides, was considerably smaller than Pompeii.

A residential street at the bottom of the ramp offers a more genteel view of provincial Roman life than does Pompeii. Sitting astride a rise that once caught the gentle bay breezes, Herculaneum was considered a therapeutic environment whose seaside villas featured long corridors built along the axis of the afternoon sun. It also offered private marinas and artwork superior to that of its companion city.

It was easy to see why eighteenth-century romantics were

enchanted with this little community alongside the Bay of Naples. In the inner courtyard of the House of Neptune and Amphitrite in the center of town is a superb example of fine mosaic. The individual stones are less than a quarter-inch square, set by an artist's hand in deep hues of Prussian blue, ochre, silver and gold. In the great gymnasium at the eastern edge of town, a one-hundred-foot swimming pool is fed by a large bronze fountain in the shape of a tree trunk. A delicately carved Hydra is twisted about the bronze trunk, water pouring from its five mouths into the pool.

The people of Herculaneum were more cultured than their plebeian neighbors from Pompeii, for this was a town populated not so much by aggressive businessmen as by retiring upper-class Romans who had already earned their fortunes elsewhere. The streets here lack the ruts that centuries of commercial cart traffic have carved out in Pompeii.

Even in its resurrected form, Herculaneum has managed to retain a more sophisticated atmosphere. The tourists, much as the common people did two thousand years ago, seem to prefer Pompeii. The dearth of visitors made it possible for an unhurried guard to show me about. We walked first along the Decumanus Maximus, the main street where Herculaneum's commerce had been restricted by town ordinance, protecting its elegant residential districts. Large stone pillars at either end of the street prevented cart traffic, creating a pleasant mall where business was undertaken in peace. An ancient sign on a corner building threatened the residents with fines or corporal punishment for littering the area.

At the eastern edge of the street stood a public fountain decorated with a bas-relief head of Hercules, by legend the founder of the town. At the western corner was the Shrine of the Augustales, the center of worship for the cult of the Roman emperor-gods.

Only a few bodies were ever found in Herculaneum, an indication that the residents had more warning than did the Pompeiians. Excavators have recently found several skeletons along the shoreline just outside of town, prompting archaeologists to speculate that Vesuvius may have killed more people at Herculaneum than previously supposed.

The guard led me halfway down the Decumanus Maximus

to the House of the Bicentenary, a name that celebrates its excavation in 1938, two centuries after Charles, King of Sicily, confirmed the discovery of the Herculaneum ruins. The house centers on a large square atrium dominated by a black-and-white mosaic floor. The building was originally the residence of a single wealthy family, but over the centuries it had been subdivided into private apartments.

"You follow," the guard said.

He led me up a stone staircase to the second floor, where he unlocked the door to a small cubicle. Inside the darkened room I could make out a crumbling wooden cabinet with a small kneeling platform in front. The guard shone his flashlight on the wall above the cabinet, where imbedded into the plaster was the outline of a crude cross that the ancient residents had removed.

The guard struggled with his English as he explained this solemn relic. "This only . . . Christian thing found at Ercolano or Pompeii."

This extraordinary Christian find confirms an early Biblical comment on the Apostle Paul's days in Campania. When brought to trial before Porcius Festus, governor of Judaea, Paul had exercised his right as a Roman citizen to appeal directly to the emperor. In A.D. 61 a corn ship named the Castor and Pollux landed at Pozzuoli, west of Naples, bearing the pious prisoner in chains.

According to the record of Acts 28:14, Paul "found brethren, and was desired to tarry with them seven days." That Biblical record, and the image of the cross once hidden in the House of the Bicentenary, are evidence that at least some Christians were among the victims of the eruption of A.D. 79.

From the House of the Bicentenary I walked along the middle street of the three north-south roads that divide the town, pausing at various buildings to view carbonized furniture, doors, foodstuffs and utensils that the hot mud of Vesuvius had almost perfectly preserved.

Despite its superior cultural heritage, Herculaneum seems destined to remain eclipsed by Pompeii. It suffers from having been discovered first, when the techniques of excavation and archaeology were crude. Many of the finds were removed from their natural site, and although much of the art of Herculaneum can be seen today at the National Museum of Naples, its absence from the natural context is a tragedy. Some day Herculaneum may regain the eminence it held before the discovery of Pompeii, for unlike Pompeii, which is three-fourths excavated, considerable portions of Herculaneum still lie untouched beneath the contemporary village of Resina.

The streets of Herculaneum run north from the Decumanus Maximus into a barrier of rock and hardened mud. There are noble archaeological and artistic secrets buried here, but it has proved politically impossible to raze the slums of Resina above the excavations to extend the digging. Perhaps preserved in its Vesuvian mud are more scrolls of Greek and Roman literature such as those found at the Villa of the Papyri. In 1752, in this ancient villa, excavators found a library of carbonized classical works written on papyrus scrolls.

"Can you show me where the papyri were found?" I asked the guard.

He led me into the House of Aristides where in a back area of the house, illuminated only by a bare light bulb, were the mouths of several tunnels sealed off with concrete. "The Villa of the Papyri is three hundred meters off somewhere in that direction," the guard said, gesturing with his hand toward the slums of Resina. "It was covered over by the excavators more than two hundred years ago. We don't know exactly where it is, but you can see the papyri."

"Where?" I asked.

"They are in the National Library. At Naples."

The first attempts to unroll the Herculaneum papyri in the mid–eighteenth century resulted in disaster. The charred rolls disintegrated at a touch and several were lost forever. The remaining papyri sat unrolled until Father Antonio Piaggi, custodian of the Vatican Library, sent word to King Charles of Naples that he had invented a machine to do the job. He was immediately invited to the palace.

His contraption was devised from a wig-making machine that operated by attaching silk threads to the edge of a papyrus roll and cautiously turning the crank. Moving at the rate of about one centimeter per hour, the machine pulled the fragile material apart, backing it onto the tissue of a pig's bladder. It was ponderous and comical, but it worked. After four years of labor, Neapolitan scholars announced that the first papyrus was a portion of *On Music* by the philosopher Philodemus.

It was a great ancient find, but a disappointment to classicists, for Philodemus proved to be merely a lesser disciple of Epicurus, not one of the great classical minds. As years passed and more papyri were unrolled it became evident that the owner of the villa was devoted to Philodemus. A few works of Epicurus were identified, but the bulk of the papyri were comparatively poor works.

The identification of Philodemus provided a clue to the villa's ownership. Philodemus was a philosopher-slave from Gadara, near the Sea of Galilee, who could not have owned such a magnificent estate. Scholars believe that this may have been the family residence of his patron, Lucius Calpurnius Piso Caesoninus, father-in-law of Julius Caesar. The great Caesar might have journeyed with his wife Calpurnia to Piso's villa near the sea at Herculaneum to discuss politics and philosophy amid the pacific Campanian summers.

Today, except for a token display at the National Museum of Naples, the papyri are locked in wooden cabinets in the recesses of the National Library, which occupies a back wing of the former Royal Palace. When I came to see them, I was greeted cordially by Professor Marcello Giganti, curator of the papyri collection. One side of the small room was taken up by laboratory tables supporting powerful microscopes. The remainder of the room was crowded with a news crew from one of Italy's two public television networks who were filming a documentary on the papyri.

"The papyri were first read in the 1700s and 1800s without the help of a microscope," Giganti explained to me. "Now we are studying them with a microscope, making corrections." Extending his hand toward a microscope, he asked, "Would you like to see?"

I sat down and removed my glasses. Giganti showed me how to focus the microscope, warning me not to touch the papyri. I stared through the twin lenses and brought into focus a dark brown ragged surface honeycombed with fibrous tears. Latin script in faded gray ink was easily distinguishable.

"Which papyrus is this?" I asked.

"It is part of *On Vices* by Philodemus."

Giganti gently moved the plate that held the papyrus so that I could see more text. The gray Latin letters sped past, carrying their messages to scholars. I sat back and put my glasses on, aware of excited chatter across the room.

"Please," Giganti said. "Read some more. They are filming you for television. We are very proud to have an American *professore* visit us."

I continued to look through the microscope at the Latin text until the film crew was finished. Giganti then took me into the next room and showed me the cabinets full of papyri. He unlocked them and pulled out several drawers, one of which contained random bits of papyri pinned down like butterfly specimens.

"These are fragments from some of the rolls that were destroyed when they first tried to unroll them," he said. "They have never been read. We are studying them, but there are hundreds and, unfortunately, they are deteriorating."

With no central heating or cooling in the old Royal Palace, the papyri freeze in the winter and bake in the summer, accelerating their destruction. A government committee has been set up to create a controlled environment, but even as they deliberate the papyri from Herculaneum continue to disintegrate.

Herculaneum's excavations and papyri provided me with a glimpse of the elegance and culture that existed in the first century A.D. But records mention other settlements in addition to Pompeii and Herculaneum that were destroyed by Vesuvius in A.D. 79. How many more lost cities lie underneath the Campanian countryside waiting for the archaeologists' shovels? Was there a community even more refined than Herculaneum still to be unearthed?

I learned that there had been a major new discovery inside the town of Torre dell' Annunziata, reputedly part of the lost city of Oplontis. The archaeologist responsible for the excavation is Alfonso de Franciscis, formerly superintendent of antiquities of Naples Province, now professor of archaeology at the University of Naples. A cultured man in his mid-sixties with a clipped gray Vandyke, de Franciscis lives in a high-ceilinged apartment overlooking the Bay of Naples, where I visited him.

De Franciscis has spent fifty years studying the ruined cities of the A.D. 79 eruption; in fact, he is the author of the guide-book I had purchased at Pompeii. Prior to his retirement a few years ago, his attention turned from Pompeii to the new site. De Franciscis explained that from the opulent nature of this buried villa, it is apparent that it was the site of another Roman resort, perhaps superior in culture and architecture to Herculaneum. No contemporary accounts of the A.D. 79 erup-tion mentioned Oplontis, he told me, but its approximate lo-cation was indicated on a thirteenth-century map known as the Peutinger Table.

"I have found a great villa there," de Franciscis said with quiet enthusiasm. "We suppose it was the home of Poppaea, the wife of the Emperor Nero." Poppaea Sabina, Nero's second wife, came from a Pompeiian family, and the villa found at Torre dell' Annunziata may have been her country estate. The supposition is based upon inscriptions that indicate ownership by the Poppaea family, and from the fact that this is the single most luxurious Roman villa ever discovered.

The villa is not yet open to the general public, but de Fran-ciscis arranged for me to visit in my door-opening guise of an American *professore*. Torre dell' Annunziata is located imme-diately off the autostrada south of Naples, between Hercula-neum and Pompeii. Yellow road signs easily directed my driver to the excavations, which cover two city blocks in the heart of a busy commercial zone of the modern town.

A guide took me into the excavation pit, where the villa occupied an area about 180 feet long and 150 feet wide sur-rounded by the remains of elegant gardens and arcades. The wealth of its owner was clearly indicated not only by the size of the villa, but by the quality of the abundant wall paintings that depicted such objects as glass fruit bowls, golden sceptres and strolling peacocks. The artwork had a delicacy of touch that far surpassed the paintings at Pompeii and Herculaneum, with intricate golden vines trailing up decorative columns, careful perspective that provided blank walls with an illusion of open space, even a transparent veil adorning a basket of fruit.

At one end of the rectangular villa was an open-air swimming pool fully the size of a modern Olympic one surrounded by scores of decorative marble busts. In the courtyard were the plaster casts of massive trunks, remains of trees spaced to create maximum shade from the warm Campanian sun.

It was not difficult to imagine Poppaea living there in splendor as her husband carried out his intrigues in Rome, but it is impossible to determine who was actually there during the eruption of A.D. 79. Poppaea died in A.D. 65, three years prior to her husband's suicide, and whether the villa was reoccupied is not known. Thus far only the body of a servant girl has been discovered.

Surrounding the classical remains I noticed the familiar strata of volcanic material, including a six-foot layer of white pumice stone, topped by six more feet of pyroclastic residue. The sight of that Vesuvian debris all about the villa brought to mind a portion of my conversation with Professor de Franciscis. I had asked: "Do you worry that all of your work at Oplontis may someday be covered up again by Vesuvius?"

De Franciscis removed his glasses and contemplated the ceiling before he answered. "You have to ask the volcanologists. They are worried, because the time is due for Vesuvius to erupt."

8

PRELUDE TO POMPEII

IF PREHISTORIC MAN had occupied the area surrounding the Bay of Naples, he might not have seen Vesuvius above the horizon. It was only sometime between seventeen thousand and two hundred thousand years ago that a series of massive underground explosions forced a new volcano to rise from the bottom of the Bay of Naples. The volcano began its life as an island, but the debris from its eruption gradually filled the bay until the new mountain, by then sixty-five hundred feet high, had joined the mainland.

The soil around the volcano became so mineral-rich it could produce three full crops per year and, when allowed to lie fallow, spontaneously generated perfumed roses. By the time of the Roman Empire, the volcano had remained dormant for one thousand years or more and it is likely that the local population had forgotten that the mountain had ever exploded. Vegetation covered its slopes and wild boars populated its quiet crater. The people of Campania, including the residents of the busy trading center of Pompeii on the River Sarno, came to regard Vesuvius as a mute observer of their ways, nothing more. Even those few Roman scholars perceptive enough to discern evidence of past volcanic eruptions were convinced that Vesuvius was now dead.

What had the prescientific scholars believed volcanoes to be? Opinions varied, but almost none clearly saw the simple geologic truth. Plato postulated a series of subterranean channels through which the four elemental substances of earth, wind, fire and air coursed in agitated rhythm. In his scenario, these hidden streams converged into a voluminous underground cavern, which Plato designated as Tartarus. From this reservoir the fiery fountain burst.

Another Greek philosopher, Empedocles, was the first to use critical observation to construct a plausible theory. After living for several years on the slopes of Mount Etna on Sicily, he came to believe that the earth's core was a molten mass. The volcano Etna, he said, was an escape vent for the internal pressures. Empedocles, according to some sources, is said to have perished by fire in Etna's crater in 432 B.C., and his manuscripts with him.

Nero's tutor, Seneca, developed a hypothesis that most closely approaches the modern explanation. He believed that volcanoes were safety valves to liberate stress, not from an incandescent global mass, but from localized reservoirs of gas and molten rock. Seneca's inventory of known volcanoes included Etna, Stromboli and Vulcano. Significantly, it did not include Vesuvius, which was ostensibly dormant at the time.

Beyond the scientific philosophy, there was another concept, that of spiritism, which seemed very real to the early Campanians. Following Greek thought, the Romans considered the underground to be the repository of the dead, where spirits survived their bodies. Since volcanoes were subterranean phenomena, the Romans interpreted the eruptions as negative messages from the spirits of the dead.

No Roman scholar could make the now-obvious connection between volcanic eruptions, earthquakes, hot springs and the smoldering sulfurous lakes that afflicted southern Italy. Rather, they believed the phenomena were the product of random whims of gods or spirits.

Strabo of Amaseia, a Greek scholar who compiled an ambitious geography about 7 B.C., was among the first to realize that Vesuvius was a volcano. Either he, or the source of his information, climbed to the summit of Vesuvius and recounted that the interior was an ash-covered hollow. Strabo reasoned: "From this we may infer that the place was formerly in the burning state with live craters." Long before the eruption of A.D. 79 he falsely concluded that Vesuvius had become "extinguished on the failing of the fuel."

He was proved wrong about Vesuvius' fuel, but unlike Strabo, the common people of Pompeii probably never even suspected that the mountain that was about to destroy them was a volcano.

According to legend, the city of Pompeii was founded by Hercules, the heroic Greek man-god and son of Zeus. The historian Diodorus of Sicily, who lived in the first century B.C., tells us that Hercules came to the Phlegraean Plain where he encountered an army of Giants and "with the help of the gods . . . slew most of the Giants, and brought the land under cultivation."

Hercules was said to have remained long enough to found two settlements, including one named after him, Herculaneum. The name of the other was said to be a reference to the pomp (both a Greek and Latin term) with which Hercules celebrated his spectacular victory. The prosaic reality may be that the name simply meant "the city of the Pompeius family," for that surname was a common one in that town near the mouth of the river Sarno. It is also possible that the name Pompeii derives from the Oscan word for "five."

In time Pompeii became a melting pot, absorbing the cultures of Italic and Greek peoples that had settled the area. The indigenous Oscans were ultimately conquered, not by force but by economics. Greek settlers began migrating there in large numbers about the eighth century B.C., and soon established flourishing trade routes along the Bay of Naples for their shipping enterprises. Over several centuries, Pompeii, Herculaneum and the other local towns, although not tied politically to Greece, became Hellenic in culture and style.

By the fifth century B.C., Campanian prosperity had become the envy of nearby Samnite societies to the east. Mountain men who entered into battle in silver and gold armor, the Samnites attacked and crushed resistance throughout much of Campania, but their rule was only a prelude to a more complete domination by Rome, which eventually conquered the entire area.

During the period of the triumvirate of Gnaeus Pompey, Marcus Crassus and Julius Caesar in the first century B.C., Pompeii was a thriving commercial city but too close to Neapolis to become a true Roman metropolis. It would have remained a footnote in Roman history except for the presence of

Vesuvius, a seemingly innocent mountain background for the city, but one that was to shape its eternal future.

Ignorance of Vesuvius' volcanic power made the crater an attractive place for military adventure, particularly if one were seeking a virtually impregnable mountain redoubt. A celebrated soldier, the slave-gladiator Spartacus, was in search of just such a refuge and he enters the story of Vesuvius through a successful invasion of its crater. Born in Thrace (modern Bulgaria), Spartacus had served in the Roman army with a corps of Thracian mercenaries, but had deserted. Forced to live as a roving thief, he was captured and consigned to the gladiator school managed by Gnaeus Lentulus Batiatus at Capua, north of Naples.

In the summer of 73 B.C., Spartacus led some two hundred fellow slaves in a plan to overthrow their Roman masters. The conspiracy was discovered prematurely, but seventy-eight insurgents managed to escape to Capua where they seized wagons carrying gladiators' arms and moved southward encountering only feeble opposition. Pursued by Roman legions, Spartacus and his men headed for Vesuvius. As the Roman historian Publius Annius Florus described it: "The first position which attracted them (a suitable one for such ravening monsters) was Mt. Vesuvius."

From the summit, Spartacus could see the crater as a basin extending a mile across, filled with a dense growth of vines. It seemed a secure hide-out, for as the Greek biographer Plutarch later explained, "there was but one ascent which was very narrow and rugged, and he [Spartacus] placed a sufficient guard." If the Romans attacked, they would have to approach the summit single file.

As news of Spartacus' rebellion spread, thousands of slaves joined him at his Vesuvian retreat. Rome sent a strike force of three thousand men, under the leadership of Claudius Glaber, to eradicate the rebels. Glaber realized that his men would have to climb the mountain to engage gladiators trained in solo combat, and decided instead to starve out the brigands. He laid siege to Vesuvius, reasoning that the only entrance was also the sole exit.

Spartacus quickly devised not only an escape route but a plan of attack against the Romans, who were camped at the very base of Vesuvius. His army used kitchen knives and swords to slash at the vines that covered the crater, then twisted them into a thick rope ladder. Plutarch chronicled their achievement:

> By the help of this ladder they all got down safe, except one. This man remained above only to let down their arms; and when he had done that he descended after them. The Romans knowing nothing of this maneuver, the gladiators came upon their rear, and attacked them so suddenly, that they fled in great consternation, and left their camp to the enemy.

Word of Spartacus' victory encouraged thousands of slaves to join the rebellion, but the insurgents had to quit Vesuvius, for Spartacus realized his daring maneuver could not be repeated. Marcus Crassus finally led an army large enough to overpower the rebels in the field. Spartacus, according to some sources, died fighting at the head of his troops. Others record that he was crucified along the Appian Way.

Little more is known of Pompeiian or Vesuvian history until February 5, A.D. 62, in the tenth year of the reign of Emperor Nero Claudius Caesar Drusus Germanicus. The Roman era had reached its zenith as all of Italy began to enjoy the prosperity of Rome's Eurasian spoils. Pompeii, as the hometown of Nero's wife, Poppaea Sabina, flourished.

On that February morning Pompeii experienced a shock that, in retrospect, was the first indication that Vesuvius was awakening after a thousand years. The events of this day were to be a prologue to a later drama, one that would transform Vesuvius from a tranquil mountain into a fearsome volcano that would simultaneously annihilate and preserve Pompeii, and, over the course of two millennia, change the face of Campania.

There are two sources of information about the events of February 5, A.D. 62: a report written by Nero's minister Seneca, and the record preserved in the twin bas-reliefs found in the home of a Pompeiian banker, L. Caecilius Jucundus.

Though one of the original reliefs has been stolen, copies exist at the National Museum of Naples. From these sources it is possible to recreate the opening scene in the tragedy of Pompeii.

That morning L. Caecilius Jucundus walked almost halfway across town to the Forum to conduct his business for the day. One of the most prosperous of Pompeiians, Jucundus presided over an extensive range of finance including real estate, commodities and banking.

In the Forum, enterprise thrived. Since chariots and horses were banned, children played safely in the arcades flanking the Temple of Jupiter while their elders concluded the morning's barter. Vendors of sausages, fruits and cakes, the so-called "people of the Forum," hawked their wares vociferously.

Jucundus happened to be facing north in the Forum around noontime, when the ground beneath his feet began to oscillate, and a stentorian crack shattered his morning tranquillity. The earth first pitched upward, then swayed as secondary waves rocked the land. To Jucundus' horror, the columns of the Temple of Jupiter toppled directly in front of him, collapsing the structure's gilded roof.

At the other end of the Forum, the Temple of Apollo buckled under the stress of the quake, crushing children in the covered arcades that flanked the plaza. Two statues of horsemen tilted precariously on their high pedestals as buildings fell around the terrified banker. As new underground waves rolled toward Pompeii from the vicinity of Vesuvius, slabs of lava pavement split open and roof tiles clattered into the crowded streets.

Jucundus raced to his home at the intersection of Via di Nola and Via di Stabia, near the north gate of town. His attention was diverted to a commotion outside the gate, where a chariot drawn by two oxen had overturned in the road. People fleeing through the gate to the open countryside moved quickly around the obstruction.

As Jucundus watched the crowd, the north gate toppled and the town reservoir collapsed, inundating the northern portion of the city with water. Jucundus struggled to his home to find that the entire upper story was demolished. He was distraught at the loss but murmured thanks to the gods for carrying him to the Forum on business that morning.

The quake had been felt throughout Campania. A few buildings collapsed in Naples, most notably the gymnasium, and Nuceria suffered slight damage. But by far the greatest toll was levied upon Pompeii and Herculaneum, where the destruction was so extensive that many questioned whether these cities in the Vesuvian foothills should be rebuilt. Few doubted that the quake was a divine rebuff, but no one could say which god had demanded retribution, or why. Some believed Jupiter was displeased, but if he was responsible, why had he leveled his own temple?

After sorting through the rubble and cremating their dead, the Pompeiians set to work rebuilding. Many homes were rehabilitated hastily, their frescoes patched together with little artistic care. Broken pottery was swept from the floors and added to fresh plaster to patch the honeycombed walls. But a decision was made to restore the public buildings with more care, altering their architectural style from subdued classical Greek to the more gaudy Roman manner. At the ruins of the Jucundus house, workmen rebuilt the collapsed upper story. In gratitude to the gods who spared his life, Jucundus commissioned the execution of twin marble reliefs depicting the awesome earthquake in exquisite detail.

The Pompeiians were unable to comprehend that the earthquake, so obviously centered near Vesuvius, was an aborted eruption of the old volcano. Dormant for one thousand years or more, its ancient vents had become clogged and solidified and only an epic cataclysm such as this earthquake could open them and reactivate the volcano.

On August 24, A.D. 79, the necessary geologic forces were in place to produce the great eruption that destroyed Pompeii. To reconstruct that drama in the proper context of new geological theory requires the integration of information from a variety of sources. That awesome day has been described in several fictional accounts, notably in Sir Edward Bulwer-Lytton's 1834 novel *The Last Days of Pompeii*, in which the entire city population was conveniently, but fancifully, placed in the great Amphitheatre.

It is now possible to draw a more realistic portrait of the eruption, using both traditional and contemporary sources. What follows is drawn from two letters from an eyewitness, a Roman, Pliny the Younger, written to the Empire's great historian Cornelius Tacitus; interviews with volcanologists in Italy and the United States; discussions with archaeologists at Pompeii, Herculaneum and the National Museum at Naples; the official written reports of the Italian excavators over a period of 120 years; and my own observations of Pompeii and its plaster impressions, the only remains of the victims who, near noontime on August 24, A.D. 79, suddenly turned in the direction of Vesuvius, from where they heard a deafening roar.

1

1. This Pompeiian portrait of a man and his wife was probably painted during the last years before the town's destruction by Vesuvius.

2. The plaster body cast of a young Pompeiian woman who died of suffocation in the A.D. 79 eruption of Vesuvius. In a vain final attempt to protect herself from the fumes and falling ash, she had pulled her tunic up over her face.

2

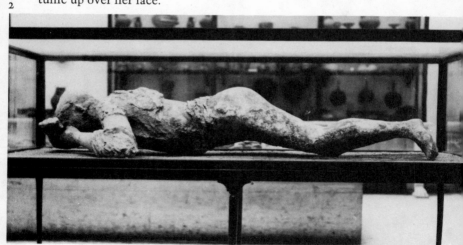

3.   4.

3. Pliny the Elder, Roman admiral and philosopher, whose death during the eruption of A.D. 79 was recorded in detail by his nephew, Pliny the Younger, in a letter to the Roman historian Tacitus.

4. Pliny the Younger at first refused to leave his home in Misenum until his uncle, Pliny the Elder, returned from a voyage on the Bay of Naples, where he hoped to rescue survivors of the great eruption of A.D. 79.

5. This bronze horse head with traces of gilding was found in the theater at Herculaneum. The excavation of the theater in 1738 was the first clue that the ancient cities destroyed by Vesuvius had been found.

5.

6

6. A contemporary engraving of the eruption of 1631. The village at the extreme right (K) is Torre del Greco, where as many as 18,000 died. Fearing the Black Plague, the unfortunate citizens remained within the city walls, where they were engulfed by boiling, watery lava.

7. The German poet Johann Wolfgang von Goethe, painted during his visit to Italy by artist Johann Tischbein. Goethe and Tischbein climbed Vesuvius together during one eruption.

7

8   9

8. Percy Bysshe Shelley visited Pompeii and Herculaneum as part of the obligatory nineteenth-century Grand Tour. He was deeply impressed by his first sight of Pompeii, but the periodic rumblings of Vesuvius cast him into melancholia. It was at Pompeii that he was inspired to write part of his classic "Ode to Naples."

9. Charles Dickens as a young man, about the time he visited Pompeii and Vesuvius. Leading a party of tourists and local people, Dickens ascended the volcano during an icy winter to see the summit by moonlight.

10. Charles Babbage, noted Cambridge mathematician and inventor of the first calculating machine, climbed forty feet down inside the live vent of Vesuvius during an eruption to test his mathematical theory of the rate of the rise and fall of the hot lava.

11. Alexandre Dumas, *père*, famed author of *The Three Musketeers*, served as Director of Excavations at Pompeii and Herculaneum in 1860, a post he received as a reward for helping Garibaldi and his army conquer Naples and reunite Italy.

10   11

12

14

13

12. Residents inspect the wreckage caused by lava in the village of Boscoreale during the 1906 eruption of Vesuvius.
13. The demolished tracks of the Circumvesuviana Railway, destroyed by lava in the eruption of 1906.
14. Villagers clear volcanic ash from the streets of Ottaviano after the 1906 eruption of Vesuvius.

15. Vesuvius and the Bay of Naples during a minor eruption of the volcano in 1930.

16

17

16. An aerial view of the central crater of Vesuvius during the eruption of 1930. A lava lake is shown in the left foreground of the crater.
17. An ash cloud sits over Vesuvius during the 1944 eruption, which took place only months after the Allied occupation of the city of Naples, shown in the foreground.
18. The author descending the steep slope into the crater of Vesuvius. He made the journey with the help of the Alpine Club of Italy.

18

9

THE DEATH OF POMPEII

IT WAS A SPECIAL DAY, the day after the birthday of Augustus, the Roman ruler who had brought peace to the empire. In the Roman reckoning of dates it was the ninth day before the calends of September; in the Gregorian calendar, it was August 24, A.D. 79. Since the celebration was a national holiday extending over several days, the courthouse was closed to legal business, but much of the normal industry continued as usual. Another holiday, ominous in retrospect, had been celebrated the day before. August 23 was the feast to the god of subterranean fire, Vulcan.

Seventeen years, six months and nineteen days had passed since the earthquake of A.D. 62. It had been a period of rebuilding, an attempt to recapture past glories. Scores of private homes, the fallen Temple of Isis, and the Amphitheatre, an impressive structure seating twenty thousand and cut into the natural slope of the southeastern portion of Pompeii, were fully reconstructed. Pompeii seemed destined to fall back into anonymity.

Though the lawyers and other leading citizens were indolent on the holiday, it was an ordinary morning for the working classes. Merchants took down the wooden shutters sheathing the façades of their shops. Carpenters gathered their tools and moved to their jobs. Street vendors set out their wares, their cries mingling with the clamor of workshops. The fullers set chamber pots in the streets to collect urine from passers-by for use in their toga-cleaning solutions.

On Strada dell' Abbondanza in the main shopping district east of the Forum, a tavern keeper opened her bar and set a kettle on its tripod over a small countertop fire. The engraving of Mercury at the entrance, featuring an enormous penis, suggested either prosperity or that the barmaids were available to render service of more than wine.

In the marketplace of the Forum itself, fishermen dumped their morning catch into a large water tank. Taxi-men took their stations outside the gates, waiting impatiently in horse-drawn carts. Slaves trudged to the quarries, where they were assigned to cut slabs of old lava for new pavement blocks and millstones. In the temple of Augustus, laborers prepared to install a statue of the new Emperor Titus, who had succeeded his father Vespasian on June 24, exactly two months before. Titus was known throughout the empire for the sack of Jerusalem in A.D. 70, when he had slaughtered one million rebellious Jews.

The day bore no special significance, except for the holiday and for small portents that were largely ignored by the complacent Pompeiians. Pompeii's provincial comfort had been disturbed some ten days before by ominous signs of Vesuvius awakening from one thousand years of inactivity. Wells went dry; cattle grazing on the mountain slopes bellowed woefully. A Pompeiian politician, Marcus Herennius, was suddenly struck dead and rumor held that he was inexplicably slain by a firebolt crashing out of a cloudless sky. The signs continued up through that morning of August 24, but they could hardly be deciphered by a prescientific community, and life went on uninterrupted.

As the morning sun climbed toward noon, Gaius Plinius Secundus, known to posterity as Pliny the Elder, rested after a modest lunch and a cold bath at his villa at Misenum, some twenty miles due west of Pompeii at the far end of the Bay of Naples. At the age of fifty-six, Pliny was a celebrated military leader, but he preferred the designation of scholar. Despite his avid study of natural history, Pliny, too, was unaware that Vesuvius was in the midst of a vital geological metamorphosis.

Pliny often rose at midnight to pass the hours of darkness communing with his books, preferring to rest at odd times during the day. As he read, he took copious notes, habitually scribbling memoranda about everything that he observed during the course of his day. Though overweight and a gourmand, Pliny disdained invitations, preferring to dine in solitude so that he might be free to read during his meal.

His nephew, Gaius Plinius Caecilius Secundus, known as Pliny the Younger, was a close observer of his uncle. He once detailed his uncle's regimen in a letter to Baebius Macer:

> In the country, he exempted only his bathing time from study; I mean, the actual time of his immersion in the water, for while he was being rubbed or dried, he would hear something read or would dictate something. While traveling, he threw aside every other care, and gave himself up to study; he always had a scribe at his side with a book and a writing tablet, whose hands in winter were protected by gloves, so that the cold weather might not rob him of a single moment. Even at Rome, he used to be carried in a litter with this view. I remember his rebuking me for taking a walk. 'You might have managed,' he said, 'not to lose these hours.'

Pliny the Elder had served the emperors Claudius, Nero, Galba, Otho, Vitellius, Vespasian, and Titus, showing extraordinary lasting power in a period of imperial intrigue. By A.D. 79, his literary output was voluminous. He had written a book on the use of the dart by cavalry, two volumes on the life of his friend Pomponius Secundus, a twenty-volume history of the Roman wars with the Germanic tribes, and a six-volume discussion of the education of an orator, entitled *The Students*.

During the reign of Nero, when literary pursuit had become suspect, he composed his eight-volume *Questions of Grammar and Style*. His *History of the State* comprised thirty-one volumes. Two years earlier, in A.D. 77, he had published his magnum opus, a *Natural History* in thirty-seven volumes, dedicated to Titus. Among Pliny's possessions were 160 volumes of extracts, written in a tiny hand on both sides of the page. He still had much he wished to accomplish.

One of his aspirations was the proper education of his nephew. The boy's father had died early and the uncle, following custom, had adopted him. Pliny the Younger and his mother, Plinia, came to live with the elder Pliny at Misenum, the cape that forms the northwest point of the Bay of Naples, where the great man was admiral of the Roman fleet. The sea air at Misenum was beneficial for Pliny the Elder, who suffered from chronic asthma.

The elder Pliny recognized a kindred inquiring mind in the youngster, though the boy was a scholar of Stoicism, the Greek philosophy that stressed reason and submission to divine will. Pliny had sent his nephew to Rome to study classical rhetoric under Quintilian, and by the time he was fourteen, the young Pliny had written a Greek tragedy. Now, at seventeen, he was under the tutelage of his uncle in the easy atmosphere of Campania.

Philosophically, both Plinys shared a fatalistic view. Pliny the Elder wrote: "There can be no doubt that conflagrations are a punishment inflicted upon us for our luxury." As a Stoic, Pliny the Younger subscribed to the prophecy that the world would one day be destroyed by fire and fall into chaos. Even the gods would perish, he believed.

At one o'clock that August afternoon, the philosophical speculations of both Plinys assumed a hideous reality. Plinia rushed into her brother's room with the news that a threatening cloud had suddenly billowed into the sky over Campania.

What was only a distant cloud in Misenum was a black shroud to the startled citizens of Pompeii, who fled into the streets to look up at a sky which had, in moments, cast a strange midday darkness over their city. The darkness hid the omnipresent profile of Vesuvius, which, unknown to the Pompeiians, had begun its fearful work. As they stared at the sky, volcanic bombs a foot or more in diameter arched across the horizon and fell into the streets. The ground convulsed underfoot while, overhead, lightning cast sinister flashes within the black cloud. A downpour began, not of rain, but of stinging pale gray stones.

Each of the superstitious Pompeiians fashioned his own explanation for the cataclysm. It was the triumphant hour of Set, Isis' enemy and ruler of darkness. Some thought that fierce flying giants once buried underneath Vesuvius by the mighty Hercules had come to rule Campania this frightful day. Others believed that Jupiter's thunderbolts were searing the land, or that the retribution of the Persian god Mithra, a favorite of the

Pompeiians, had at last arrived. It was, many were convinced, the destruction of the earth and the gods prophesied by the philosophers. In reality, it was an archetypical volcanic eruption.

The true explanation would have been of little solace to the frightened Pompeiians, each of whom faced an immediate choice. One course of action was to flee, and thousands raced through the darkened streets, their flight imperiled by volcanic bombs weighing as much as eight pounds that randomly crushed and mutilated. The storm of pumice stone, lightweight round missiles less than one inch in diameter, covered the narrow city lanes with surprising speed as Pompeiians struggled through the rising pile of debris. Some sought out one of the eight city gates, while others searched for their homes and families. Many others moved about the city haphazardly, lost in the dark.

Eighteen thousand terrified Pompeiians fled through the city gates within the first hour. Disoriented, some ran directly north toward Vesuvius and their doom. On the western edge of Pompeii, a fortunate few escaped in boats before the waters became impassable because of high winds and the shower of volcanic debris. Those who ran east outside the Porta Nola gate fled crosswind, gradually working their way out of the path of falling pumice. To the south, at a small docking settlement on the river Sarno, some found a few available boats, while others waited in taverns and shops praying for the arrival of ships to carry them off.

The alternative strategy was to stay indoors and wait for the incomprehensible peril to pass. Most who chose this course fled to their cellars to find shelter from the bombs and showering pumice. Perhaps two thousand Pompeiians remained behind, and for a time the cautious appeared to be the sensible ones. Temporarily sheltered, they escaped the missiles that exploded from the sky, as well as the constant deluge of pumice. But as they huddled together in protective groups, the debris steadily built to a depth of six feet or more outside of and on top of their homes. Escape was becoming impossible.

The priests of Isis were among those who tarried. For them, the events required no explanation. In their dogma, Set, the ruler of darkness, had overcome Osiris, the sun, at the very zenith of his voyage through the daytime sky. Only Isis could save them now. Priests removed the sacred statues of Isis and Osiris from their pedestals, shrouding them carefully. Others mustered the sacred vessels and temple treasures containing coins so new they bore the image of Emperor Titus. The stoutest among them lifted a coarse sack into which his companions stuffed the religious materials.

In the communal dining room at the rear of the temple, other priests struggled with the sacred treasure, the life-size idol of their goddess Isis. They lifted the heavy statue from its base and dragged it across the floor toward the doorway. Suddenly their faith wavered, belief in an afterlife giving way to mortal fear. Something dark and incalculable caused them to abandon Isis at the doorway and run in terror.

Pliny the Elder climbed to a high vantage point in his villa at Misenum to better view the remarkable cloud that had now appeared over the Campanian countryside. It took the shape of a flat-topped pine, or a mushroom, rising with a thick straight trunk to a great height, then dispersing outward. The cloud was so dense that Pliny could not determine its source with accuracy.

As admiral of the Misenum fleet, Pliny ordered a ship made ready, and invited his nephew to join him in a closer examination of this startling phenomenon. Pliny the Younger declined, for he was hard at work on a study project and, as a Stoic, he was largely unconcerned with happenstance since he could not control nature.

As the older man was leaving for the harbor of Misenum, he was brought a note. History has left us two versions of its contents. It was either from Rectina, wife of Cascus, whose house was at the foot of the mountain near Herculaneum, or from a garrison of Roman soldiers at Resina, a military base also near the city. In either event, the note pleaded for rescue. Wheezing from his exertions in the dusty air, the asthmatic Pliny gathered his notebooks and hurried to the naval base.

He ordered his ship into the peril, alternately shouting commands to his crew and dictating memoranda to his scribe. Approaching land, the admiral could see that the coastline near Herculaneum had inexplicably changed. In front of him was a shallow harbor strewn with a thickening layer of rubble from the volcano. Since it was clearly impossible to dock, Pliny's pilot pleaded with his commander to return to the safety of Misenum.

Pliny wavered. It was obvious that the people on shore were beyond assistance at this time, but the curious sea might soon correct its level and he could make port long enough to take on survivors. The solemn concern of Roman government, if not always its practice, was the welfare of its citizens and Pliny the Elder could not abuse the trust.

Noting that a strong wind drove the cloud southward directly across Pompeii and farther down the coastline, Pliny grew concerned that his friend Pomponianus, who lived at Stabiae, just south of Pompeii, might be endangered. Stabiae had formerly been a thriving competitor of Pompeii for the local sea trade, but it was razed by the Roman general Lucius Cornelius Sulla in 90 B.C. after Stabiae joined a revolt against Rome. Since then the area had been populated mainly by wealthy Romans who had built majestic villas overlooking the bay, one of which was owned by Pomponianus. Pliny decided to sail for Stabiae and first rescue Pomponianus, hoping the sea would then subside and he could cruise back up the coast to aid the citizens of Pompeii and Herculaneum.

"Fortune favors the brave," Pliny told his pilot. "Conduct me to Pomponianus."

The galley altered course to the south, slipping through the channel between the mainland and the island of Capri. When he arrived at Stabiae, the admiral found his friend ready to flee, but Pliny now seemed unaffected by the panic that had overtaken Campania. He realized that he was perfectly positioned to observe and record the unusual phenomenon.

Here, south of Pompeii, the fall of pumice was substantial but not critical, and Pliny could see no immediate hazard to life. He embraced Pomponianus, reassuring him that Stabiae was safe from the volcano, and requested a bath. In the midst of the eruption, he enjoyed his luxury and afterward, refreshed, he and Pomponianus dined together quietly. Pliny's casual approach to the strange events of the day had calmed the household. During the evening hours Pliny and Pomponianus observed "broad sheets of fire and leaping flames" blazing down from Vesuvius, their luminosity emphasizing the night's blackness.

When the eruption began, Lucius Herennius Florus was at his country villa on the southern slope of Vesuvius, two miles closer to the volcano than Pompeii, at the present site of Boscoreale. The villa had been heavily damaged in the earthquake of A.D. 62, but the farm workers' quarters had recently been made usable so that the fields could be tilled and wine production resumed.

By nightfall, the residents of the villa had gathered the household treasure, a thousand gold pieces and a precious collection of silver plate. Among the silver items was a wine cup, etched with the outline of a skeleton. An inscription advised: "Enjoy life while you have it, for tomorrow is uncertain."

Everyone in the villa was ready to leave, but they hesitated when the eruption seemed to abate, ending the stinging fall of pumice. There was a respite at the mountain four miles away, but it was brief and misleading. Sometime after sunset Vesuvius exploded again in a fresh paroxysm of fire. This time the composition of the volcanic product had changed: The pumice was gone, replaced by sticky volcanic ash that blasted south along the prevailing wind currents. It was accompanied by a base surge, the enormous reservoir of molten rock and superheated water vapor crashing out from Vesuvius as a horizontal shock wave, which sped along the ground in the direction of Pompeii.

Gathering up debris as it moved at sixty miles per hour, this scorching base surge overcame all obstacles in its path, natural or man-made, as it carved a course southward. The surge leveled trees and walls perpendicular to its flow while lethal clouds of gas carrying sulfuric and hydrochloric acids accompanied the moving mass. Anyone in its path would remain there forever.

Alarmed by the new explosion of Vesuvius, a man in the Florus villa rushed to the wine cellar to hide the sack of silver and coins. Reaching the vat where grape juice was stored after pressing, he placed the treasure inside moments before he was felled by the base surge.

Above him, the mistress of the villa and her steward fled to the courtyard, uncertain in which direction to run. The man and woman placed cloths over their faces as a protection against the noxious gases, but the gesture failed to stop the suffocating effects of the volcano.

Just outside the Porta Ercolana on the north side of the city walls of Pompeii, eight people had taken refuge in the Villa of the Mysteries. Three women were huddled in an upper room when the surge hit, smashing the outer gates of the villa and shearing off its walls. When the room collapsed, the women were thrown to the lower floor. Several others who had taken shelter in the wine cellar perished at the same moment. One man, probably the villa's steward, hid in the small watchroom near the main entrance, the little finger of his left hand bearing an iron ring with an engraved stone chalcedony depicting a small female figure. He was gazing at it when he died.

A short distance further from Vesuvius, down the Via dei Tombe, twenty people hid in the Villa of Diomed, eighteen of them in the narrow wine cellar on the north side of the garden. The wine merchant and his steward chose this moment for a desperate escape attempt. Racing across the carpet of pumice in the garden, they headed for the back gate in the direction of the sea. At the instant of death the merchant's hands were thrusting the key into the lock of the gate. His servant fell behind him, holding a sack of useless treasure.

The cellar below the villa became a tomb, sealed off by volcanic material. Death came quickly to the eighteen people, many of whom drew their cloaks over their faces to ward off the burning gases. One woman survived moments longer than the others, desperately clawing her way toward the door.

In the city itself, many guests at Fabio Rufo's impressive hotel were unfamiliar with the layout of Pompeii. Afraid of becoming lost in the confusion outside, they chose to remain inside the hotel, seeking refuge in its lower floors. Vesuvius proved to be a capricious killer. Victims in the very same rooms apparently died from various causes, some from fumes, others from the weight of a collapsing roof. In one hotel room a man died on his stomach with a cloth over his nose while his companion, lying on his back, fought against the mass of the ceiling that had fallen upon his chest.

In a nearby room in the same hotel, a young family had

clasped one another in fear. When the hotel's overloaded roof fell in upon itself, the two top floors collapsed upon the family. The father was thrown upon his back, raising himself slightly on one arm in a final futile effort. His wife and three-year-old boy died at his side. Only the baby survived for a moment, crawling upward through a shaft in the midst of the debris, until existence was ended.

The base surge raced across the full width of Pompeii, simultaneously obliterating hundreds of victims caught on the northern edge of town. At the House of the Faun on Via della Fortuna east of Fabio Rufo's hotel, a woman had gathered a golden snake bracelet, rings, earrings, hairpins, a precious silver mirror and a bag of coins. When her home fell in under the assault of the surge, her possessions scattered about her. In death, the woman's outstretched arms attempted to ward off the final blow.

Further toward the eastern side of town, the Via della Fortuna becomes Via di Nola. Here many were annihilated as they raced for the northeastern gate, Porta Nola. Eight bodies fell in the middle of the street, all with their jaws open in silenced screams. Immediately outside Porta Nola a solitary man scrambled to climb a tree as the volcanic surge roared toward him. He grasped at the lower branches too late, and was thrown to the ground, still clutching the limb.

The surge moved on relentlessly through Pompeii and reached Strada dell' Abbondanza, the busy mercantile street immediately south of the center of town. Here, in the house of the Cryptoporticus, eight people hid in the wine cellar. As the surge approached, they ran for the backyard garden, where they died, one mother curled on her side cradling the head of her young daughter.

One block south, at the House of Menander, a cartload of wine stood outside the front entrance, abandoned by tradesmen who were delivering it when Vesuvius erupted. The residents of the house were less fortunate. The steward, Quintus Poppaeus Erotus, a freedman, remained in the atrium to guard the family property while other servants remained fearfully in their rooms.

Anxious hours were punctuated by the rhythmic swaying of the structure as the supporting earth heaved. Pumice billowed in through the compluvium, the opening above the atrium, and piled up inside the house. Only after the pumice had accumulated as high as the steward himself, did Vesuvius signal their final doom. Ten servants tried to break through the clogged compluvium, one leading the way with a bronze lamp. They forced their way up to the roof and down a flight of steps to the street, only to be overwhelmed by volcanic material.

Erotus made no attempt to flee. Hearing the terrible explosion, he laid his daughter gently upon her bed in their small room near the entrance of the house. Father and child pulled soft pillows over their heads and waited for oblivion. They died where they lay, Erotus faithfully clutching his master's purse and seal.

In the southwestern quadrant of Pompeii near the Porta Stabia, the land slopes off sharply. Two theatres were cut into the hillside, and behind them an old gymnasium had been converted into barracks for gladiators. Thirty-four gladiators died in one room, having decided to band together against a foe they could not openly battle. In the storage room, where armor and helmets were kept, seventeen men perished alongside a bejeweled society mistress who had chosen this morning for a final tryst with her slave-lover. A horse lay dead in the stable next to its bronze saddlery. The body of a newborn baby lay stuffed into an earthen jar in a corner room, abandoned by its fleeing mother.

The surge reached the lowest part of Pompeii, the southeast corner, perhaps a minute after it had entered the north side of town, facing Vesuvius. The great public gymnasium next to the Amphitheatre had become a refuge for many. At the onset of the eruption a crew of carpenters had abandoned their tools and retreated into a latrine under the portico at the southern edge of the complex. They barred the door to their sanctuary, perhaps fearing a rush from a mob of teen-age boys who had been surprised in the midst of their games. In their panic, the carpenters left their mule driver outside. He curled inside his blanket, where he lay for eternity, his mule dead alongside him. His companions met the same destiny, for there was no refuge in the gymnasium, or anywhere.

Having annihilated a city of twenty thousand inhabitants, the base surge was still not exhausted by the time it reached the south wall of Pompeii, some six miles from the volcano. Many had fled south, away from Vesuvius, to a small fishing suburb only a third of a mile south of Pompeii, where a flotilla of boats foundered uselessly in the churning waters of the Sarno River.

Pompeiians milled about the docks, clutching their jewels, imploring their gods. Several clustered about a small thermopolium, a hot-wine shop, where the image of a bearded sea-god offered hope. Two men stood at the bar raising a final draught of wine as death arrived. When the onslaught had ended, thirteen adults and a child died at the shop, sprawled among their useless charms to the goddess of Fortune. Scores of other bodies lay strewn along the street of the dockside settlement.

More than six miles from the vent of Vesuvius, the surge finally lost its potency. Later explosions covered Pompeii with layers of volcanic rock mixed with thickening ash, but by then Pompeii and the Pompeiians were already dead.

That night, a series of sharp earth tremors awakened Pliny the Younger at his uncle's villa at Misenum. He leaped from his bed and raced to find his mother, Plinia. The seventeen-year-old scholar had remained with his books throughout the eventful afternoon, then bathed, dined and napped, only to be awakened by shocks that overturned the furniture in his room. All night long mother and son sat in the open courtyard safely away from walls that threatened to collapse. Stoicism, which preached human inability to control external events, strengthened young Pliny's serenity. In the midst of that terrible night he called for a volume of Livy and continued to read while Vesuvius raged.

An older man visiting from his government post in Spain, a friend of Pliny's uncle, rushed into the courtyard during the night and rebuked Plinia for being patient with a son who meditated while peril increased. The visitor counseled immediate flight, but the boy still ignored the advice, returning his thoughts to his book.

At Pomponianus' villa at Stabiae, Pliny the Elder had insisted upon a nap despite threatening flames to the north. He retired to a small bedroom off the peristyle, and to the astonishment of others, the sound of his untroubled snoring could soon be heard.

Pomponianus remained awake through the night, watching the perilous shower of volcanic debris fill his courtyard. Stabiae was too far south to be leveled by a base surge, and the volume of pumice and ash was less than that in Pompeii, but it was potent enough that by morning the doorway to Pliny's bedroom was partially blocked.

A worried Pomponianus awakened his friend before escape became impossible. As the villa swayed from violent quakes, Pliny and Pomponianus debated whether to remain inside or risk flight outdoors. They chose the latter, then strapped pillows to their heads and hastened into the unnaturally dark morning, servants leading the way with torches and lamps. The party moved toward the beach, but the sea was still too frenzied to launch boats to reach Pliny's waiting ship. When the old philosopher complained of difficulty in breathing, someone spread a blanket for him to lie upon. Pliny asked for cold water as sulfur fumes burned his asthmatic throat.

He lay there for several minutes before a burst of volcanic fury terrorized the entire group. As flames and fumes approached Stabiae, Pliny rose to flee with the others. He leaned heavily upon two slaves for a moment and then collapsed to the ground. Pliny the Elder was dead, a victim of acrid fumes or of a sudden heart seizure.

Unaware of his uncle's death, Pliny the Younger felt his first real sense of anxiety at dawn. The breeze had carried most of the debris southward, but the ash cloud was so copious that some of it moved north against the wind toward the younger Pliny at Misenum, staining the morning sky a charcoal gray.

Pliny and his mother carefully inspected the damage inflicted on their villa during the evening earthquakes. They found cracks undermining the walls surrounding the courtyard. As a precaution, they left the house and stepped out onto the road where they were soon surrounded by refugees. By torchlight some of their neighbors recognized the young Pliny and implored him to lead them from destruction. Pliny resisted, explaining that he hoped his uncle's galley would soon reappear; he did not want to leave Misenum before the admiral returned.

His uncle's friend, the diplomat from Spain, addressed Pliny: "If your uncle is alive, he wishes you to be saved. If he has perished, he certainly wished you to survive him. If so, why do you hesitate to escape?"

Young Pliny was still not persuaded, but as the morning progressed a massive black cloud scissored by lightning descended upon Misenum, first barring the view of the offshore islands, then obscuring the promontory only a short distance away. Reluctant to flee because of her age and weight, Plinia pleaded with her stoical son to escape. "I would be content to die if I did not bring death upon you," she cried.

Despite his fatalism, Pliny knew that further delay was impractical. He took his mother by the hand and led her away from the house, ignoring her complaints that she was slowing his progress. They moved toward open country, as the Vesuvian ash cloud behind them continued to spread outward.

"Let us turn out of the way while we can still see," Pliny suggested. He feared that if the cloud enveloped them and obscured all light, they would be trampled by others fleeing along the same road. Mother and son found a place to rest next to the road as the cloud wrapped them in blackness. Some near them prayed to the gods for their salvation, but Pliny no longer had faith in any gods. He took comfort in his belief that if he was about to perish, so was the rest of the world.

At the onset of the eruption, multitudes from Herculaneum, the fashionable seaside resort five miles west of Vesuvius, fled toward the nearby bay. Herculaneum's richest homes were built against the shore, some with private boat docks.

It was here at the water's edge that the residents of Herculaneum clustered, many shielding their heads with roof tiles shaken loose by the shifting earth. The earthquakes accompanying the eruption had caused the waters of the bay to recede, leaving fish floundering in the mud. Clearly the Roman galleys commanded by Pliny the Elder could not negotiate the shallow coast to rescue the residents.

At first, Vesuvius seemed to spare Herculaneum. Some

pumice and ash showered the town, but the prevailing wind carried most of the debris south toward Pompeii, granting the people of Herculaneum time to flee. A few remained at the shore, but thousands turned north toward Naples along the congested roadways. There were only a few in Herculaneum who would not, or could not, take flight.

One of these was a man at the Shrine of the Augustales on the Decumanus Maximus, the main avenue of the town. The priests of this cult, dedicated to the worship of Augustus Caesar and the succession of Roman emperor-gods, had abandoned their solemn duties and fled. They left behind one man in a small but elegant room at the rear of the shrine. He may have been a political prisoner exiled from Rome, too prominent a person to be treated as a common criminal. Iron bars on a small window prevented his escape and he could only stare at the cloud hovering over Campania. In despair he threw himself face down upon his bed.

A man and a woman who had remained behind in the Forum baths of Herculaneum took refuge in the men's dressing room, a cavernous chamber with a vaulted ceiling. Climbing onto a marble bench that curved around three sides of the room, they drew themselves up to an overhead shelf.

A teen-age boy, possibly too ill to be moved despite the volcanic threat, had been left in the home of a local jeweler. The boy spent the afternoon listening to Vesuvius roar. His parents undoubtedly had tried to reassure him before they fled. But if there was no danger, why had they left Herculaneum?

All night, masses of magma and surface rock dislodged from the long occluded vent burst from Vesuvius and collected in depressions on the upper slopes of the mountain. Reservoirs of subterranean water then came into contact with the magma chamber, propelling enormous geysers of steam skyward. The water vapor condensed upon contact with the air and fell back to earth as violent cloudbursts, which saturated the countryside with hot, hellish rain. The storms then beat down upon the accumulating heap of rubble on the upper slopes of the mountain, forming a mixture of rocky, viscous mud.

Sometime after the eruption had destroyed Pompeii, a final paroxysm on the western edge of the summit of Vesuvius shook free this ocean of mud. Sliding slowly at first, gathering

momentum as it moved downslope following the natural contours of the land, the avalanche of earth seemed to take precise
aim on Herculaneum. It moved rapidly, at thirty miles per
hour, collecting debris as it advanced, finally building to a
forty-foot crest.

The avalanche of mud approached Herculaneum, then
swept through its defenseless streets, burying everything in its
path. The colonnade of the great theatre was shattered. Bronze
statues were crushed, their fragments mixed into the warm
cauldron of mud. Two lifeless bodies floated upward in the
muck, rising twenty-five feet above the street level. The onslaught of earth reached the Shrine of the Augustales and engulfed the unfortunate prisoner. Two attendants at the Forum
baths, clinging to a high ledge in the men's dressing room,
were encased in the wet earth. The jeweler's son was entombed alongside the bones of the chicken he had eaten for
lunch.

The volcanic wave of earth passed effortlessly over Herculaneum and reached the shore of the bay, thrusting two
hundred yards out into the water before it stopped. In only a
few moments, the small but cultured Roman town of Herculaneum was transformed into a desolate mound of lifeless volcanic slime.

Pliny the Younger and his mother sat in isolation for hours
by the side of the road not far from Misenum. It was the end of
the second day of the eruption, and the blackness began to give
way to the soft light of afternoon as the ash cloud receded
slowly before a strengthening wind. Pliny, resigned to the end,
was surprised to see the sun emerge. The light revealed the
first view of Vesuvius since the eruption began, and the survivors sat transfixed by the sight of their tormentor.

Like the Campanian countryside, the volcano had been torn
apart. Two-thirds of its majestic cone was gone, leaving only a
circling ridge on the side facing Naples. A new cone had risen
near the center of the old mountain, giving Vesuvius a double
summit.

Pompeii itself was covered with twenty feet of stone and ash
with only the tops of the highest buildings protruding from
the ruins. Gone too were the towns of Herculaneum, Stabiae,

Oplontis, Taurania, Tora, Sora, Cossa and Leucopetra, and the magnificent suburban villas that had covered the lower slopes of Vesuvius. Perhaps two thousand bodies were entombed at Pompeii. Thousands of others, who had found the open terrain no more of a refuge than the city, now lay dead in the countryside.

Pliny and his mother returned to the villa at Misenum, where they anxiously awaited news of their uncle and brother. Three days after the eruption, the body of Pliny the Elder was found near the Stabian shore, the most distinguished victim of the most memorable volcanic eruption in civilized history.

10

THE MOUTH OF HELL

HESITANTLY, OVERCOME WITH GRIEF, the survivors of Pompeii returned to gaze at the destruction wrought by Vesuvius. The area encompassing Pompeii was desolate, the tops of the tallest buildings protruding through a smothering blanket of ash, pumice and cooling pyroclastic rock.

Gone was the haughty Temple of Jupiter, the king of the gods whose strength was useless against the onslaught of natural might. Apollo, Venus and the mystical Isis suffered a similar humiliation. The Forum was a wasteland; the Amphitheatre lay beneath an oval depression in the earth.

Despite the holocaust, few of the survivors could see any reason for leaving their beloved Campania. They did not understand that geologic catastrophes were due to systematic earth processes that would continue to threaten their lives. Pompeii and Herculaneum were beyond rehabilitation, but new villages, the predecessors of San Sebastiano, Torre del Greco, Portici and Boscoreale, were soon established on the slopes of Vesuvius, many uncomfortably closer to the volcano than Pompeii itself.

The Emperor Titus directed the Roman Senate to choose special consuls by lot to journey to Campania to supervise relief and reconstruction, financed, in part, by the properties of those who had perished without heirs. Titus granted special economic privileges to the cities of Neapolis (Naples), Nola, Capua and Surrentum (Sorrento), which sheltered thousands of refugees. Not content with publicly financed measures, the benevolent emperor also contributed heavily from his private treasury.

Though no one built directly atop Pompeii, many of the survivors returned to salvage what they could of their buried possessions. They had to compete with thieves who energetically searched the ruins for plunder by tunneling downward through the tops of exposed structures and then through the side walls. Working by torchlight, they made off with money, jewels, statues, household furnishings, even tile mosaics.

One of the scavengers, probably a Christian convert or a Jew, scrawled "Sodoma Gomora" on a household wall, a pronouncement that the destruction of Pompeii by Vesuvius was an angry Jehovah's retribution for the city's blatant immorality. In another home someone left the inscription "house broken into." More ominous, in a third location, was the notation: "After the ruin. . . . Where 50 were living, now after they're lying stretched . . ."

It remained for the survivors to address the question of "Why?" Since there was little scientific theory to draw upon, they looked to the gods and demons whom they must have displeased. In a third-century history of the empire, the Roman senator Dio Cassius Cocceianus blended fact with the ancient myth that Hercules had once buried a race of giants beneath Vesuvius. The giants, Dio Cassius believed, had burst forth from the volcano, causing the catastrophic eruption. He even reported that some of the eyewitnesses had seen gargantuan forms flying over Vesuvius that fateful day.

Those Romans who had come to believe in the Judeo-Christian god of Jehovah saw the disaster as divine retribution for the sins of Rome, particularly its destruction of the Temple of Solomon in Jerusalem only nine years before the Vesuvian eruption. A mysterious prophecy was circulated in the Sibylline Books that is purported to have been written prior to A.D. 79:

When the fire escaping from the broken earth of Italy reaches the open sky, it will burn many cities and kill many men; the wide sky will be full of ashes while drops like ochre fall. Recognize then the wrath of gods in heaven; because they will destroy the innocent tribe of the pious.

The Sibylline Books, scholars now know, were largely composed by Hellenized Jews who commented upon contemporary events as though they had been previously prophesied. The eruption was considered punishment for those who would destroy the "pious," a reference to Titus' sack of Jerusalem.

Near the end of the second century A.D., the Emperor Septimus Severus, a patron of the arts, ordered further salvage work upon the desolate site of Pompeii. Since hope of rebuilding the city had by now been abandoned, workmen were sent to dig in the Forum area, retrieving large public statues and removing valuable marble slabs for new construction elsewhere. Pompeii became a quarry, a source of building materials for other towns. The tops of structures still visible after the eruption gradually disappeared as their materials were salvaged. Plant growth inexorably covered the land.

During these years Vesuvius was restless. The historical record is scant, but there apparently was a violent seven-day eruption in the reign of Severus, about A.D. 203, which curtailed the salvage work. Dio Cassius indicated that the volcano remained in agitation some two centuries after the fall of Pompeii. He wrote:

The mountain Vesuvius stands over against Naples near the sea and has unquenchable springs of fire. . . . The outlying heights of it support both trees and vines—many of them—but the crater is given over to fire and sends up smoke by day, flames by night . . . This goes on all the time, sometimes more, sometimes less.

The destruction that had befallen Pompeii within two days now began to overtake the Roman Empire itself, beset by political intrigue, overburdened by governing an extended domain, and pinched by a declining economy. Constantine the Great shifted the seat of his government to Byzantium (in modern Turkey) in the year 330. He renamed the city Nova Roma, though his successors persisted in calling it Constantinople.

Though the Roman emperors had fled to Constantinople, Vesuvius still managed to plague them across the Mediterranean. In November 472, an explosion bellowed from the interior of the mountain, creating a pine-shaped cloud of ash. Strong winds pushed the cloud eastward, draping a fine white blanket, four inches thick, on Constantinople, seven hundred miles distant. Emperor Leo fled the Byzantine capital, returning only when the volcano quieted.

He ordered that thereafter there was to be an annual prayer festival to ward off another Vesuvian eruption. Leo's prayers were unanswered; the mountain continued its activity. Procopius, private secretary to the Byzantine general Belisarius, became acquainted with Vesuvius when he accompanied the army on its Italian campaign against the Ostrogoths from 536 to 540 and left us a vivid account of the volcano's violence:

> And if anyone travelling on the road is caught by this terrible shower, he cannot possibly survive, and if it falls upon houses, they too fall under the weight of the great quantity of ashes. . . . Formerly this rumbling took place, they say, once in a hundred years or even more, but in later times it has happened much more frequently.

For those who still lived alongside the great mountain during these years, life became a bleak, tenuous existence. The Roman Empire was little more than rubble, breeding an atmosphere of decay in which there seemed to be no reason to preserve the memory of Vesuvius' victims. Soon, there was no trace left of the Roman cities destroyed in the eruption of A.D. 79.

Three centuries had passed after the birth of Jesus Christ before the new religion replaced the Greco-Roman gods completely. The spread of Christianity among the Romans was continual, but it was regularly interrupted by bloody persecutions of new converts. Under the urging of his adopted son Galerius, the Emperor Diocletian began a severe attack on Christians in February 303, one that lasted for eight years and brought about the torturous deaths of some fifteen hundred believers.

The religious martyrdom of one of these victims is curiously intertwined with the story of Vesuvius. In Pozzuoli, during the height of Diocletian's oppression, a large group of Christian believers were condemned to be devoured by wild beasts. Gennaro, the Christian bishop of Beneventum, twenty-five miles northeast of Naples, came to comfort them, but he too was seized and marked for death. It is said that when the believers, including Gennaro, were thrown to the beasts, the animals refused to attack, forcing Roman troops to behead the Christians instead.

The bishop of Beneventum has since been elevated to sainthood as San Gennaro, the city patron of Naples, where his cathedral has become the religious center of Campania. To the devout, Gennaro has always been the saint whose ministrations protect the people from the evil of Vesuvius.

One Sunday I attended Mass at the Cathedral of San Gennaro in central Naples to learn more about this resolute saint. I was early for the main service, but on time for the 10:30 Mass in the small Chapel of San Gennaro off the main hall. The intimate sanctuary centered on an ornate silver altar guarded by cherubs, and a large bronze sculpture of San Gennaro. The saint was seated, his right arm upraised in blessing. Subdued lighting accented silver scrollwork, gilded candlesticks and an open Bible atop the altar. Shortly after I took my seat, a bell chimed in the distance, signaling the arrival from a side door of Father Giuseppe Morelli, *Abbate* of San Gennaro, a small man who was lost in a flapping white robe and golden coverlet.

After a short Mass, Father Morelli guided me to his inner office where he told me the story of his saint, smoking as he talked. "A pious woman managed to save some of San Gennaro's blood in a bottle after he was beheaded," Father Morelli explained. "Some time later the bishop of Naples went to Pozzuoli to get the body, and the woman gave him the blood, which had dried. As they were taking the body to Naples, the blood miraculously turned liquid."

Each year on the anniversary of that event, the first Saturday of May, and again on the anniversary of the saint's death, September 19, the sacred vial of dried blood is unlocked from its cubicle in the chapel altar by the mayor of Naples. He keeps one key to the cubicle and Father Morelli holds the other. The Abbate reverently clutches the golden handle of what looks like a clear hand mirror, inside of which the coagulated blood of San Gennaro is visible. Worshippers begin to pray, then continue their supplications until the blood suddenly turns liquid. "The miracle takes place in my hands!" Father Morelli told me in an awed voice. "Usually it happens after twenty or thirty minutes of prayer. Sometimes it takes several hours."

It is a miracle fervently desired by the devout, for if the blood fails to liquefy it is a sinister omen. Some say that on those rare occasions when San Gennaro delays, a group of women seated in the front rows begin to hurl vile epithets at the saint, but Father Morelli denies this. "They pray in a very violent way, but it isn't true that they call him names."

The Abbate showed me the red leather journals in which he and his predecessors have kept careful records of the miracle of liquefaction over the centuries. Because San Gennaro is called upon to perform his miracle whenever Vesuvius threatens, the tradition of San Gennaro's blood provides an index to what would otherwise be unknown eruptions. In the absence of scientific observations, the Roman Catholic Church was the only body to record the activities of Vesuvius. By concerning itself with the religious implications of its seemingly diabolic fire, the church has fashioned a priceless volcanic history.

Church records indicate that in 685 the Campanian countryside was devastated by an earthquake felt for thirty miles around. The shock was followed by lava that gushed from Vesuvius and descended upon the surrounding plain. In Naples, the relics of San Gennaro were hurriedly paraded in the streets amidst rumors that the saint himself was seen flying above the volcano, personally quelling the threatening flames. The event was later seen by some as a portent of the death of Pope Benedict II on May 8 of the same year.

There was a further eruption in 993, about which almost nothing is known other than a brief notation in the chronicles of the monk Glabrus Rudolphus. On February 27, 1036, Vesuvius again exploded. Sketchy reports mention that fissures opened in the side of the mountain, releasing a flood of lava that scorched a pathway to the edge of the Bay of Naples, four miles away. Only ten years later, in 1046, Vesuvius erupted again, disgorging a remarkable quantity of lava, described by

Cardinal Marsicano of Ostia as "a torrent of sulfurous resin or bitumen, that descended to the sea and became petrified."

In these pious times, the natural processes of geology, physics and chemistry were easily explained as the evidences of the eternal struggle between good and evil. Churchmen were relatively accurate observers of Vesuvius, but any less-than-divine explanation for its activity was heresy. There seemed to be a simple, indisputable theological interpretation for the eruption of volcanoes.

Everyone knew that the center of the earth was the location of the unfathomable fires of Hell, where the damned burned in eternal torment. Since volcanoes spouted fire from these infernal regions, they obviously were the entranceway to the land of the damned, from which there were no exits. Since Vesuvius was the only volcano near the seat of the Roman Church, it became widely regarded by the faithful as the very Mouth of Hell. If one needed further proof, could he not listen to the sounds of Vesuvius during an eruption and realize that they were the shrieks and groans of the suffering dead?

A letter written in approximately 1060 from Cardinal B. Pietro Damiano to Pope Nicholas II related stories that gave credence to the theory of a volcanic hell. Damiano reported that when a prince of Palermo visited Naples he observed the volcano spew fire and brimstone. Surely, the prince said, this was an omen that some rich man was about to die and be cast into these flames of Hell. The prince was reported to have died that very night.

Damiano also told the story of a priest traveling to Naples who had left his ailing mother behind at Beneventum. As he passed near Vesuvius in eruption and was awed by the fiery spectacle, he heard the voice of his own mother, moaning pitifully amid the flames. He noted the time. When he returned home he discovered it had been the very hour of her death.

The pious of the period were drawn to the mountains of the countryside, including Vesuvius, as fitting places in which to dedicate their lives to the contemplation of holiness. Monasteries and convents were erected at various isolated mountain outposts, and a hermitage was established on the northern slope of Vesuvius, about halfway down from the summit near the site of the present observatory.

After 1060, Vesuvius did not erupt for some years. Then, on May 29, 1138, according to an anonymous writer from the Convent of Monte Casino, "the mountain Vesuvius threw out fire for 40 days." By 1139 the great crater of Vesuvius was filled by internal eruptions. According to Falcone Beneventano, secretary to Pope Innocent II, Vesuvius exploded so furiously that year that the concave crater emptied completely, leaving a deep cavernous hole, and sending up a cloud that showered Campania with ash for a month.

Then, in an instant of geological time, Vesuvius once more fell quiet. All signs of smoke, so continuous in past centuries, disappeared. The Campanians remained apprehensive for a time, but they grew complacent as years passed. Vegetation covered the old lava flows as ash from past conflagrations made the earth especially fertile for grapes, olive trees and a variety of produce. Envious of the land, local farmers gradually cultivated crops higher and higher on the peaceful slopes, bringing their cattle to graze peacefully in the flat plain between Vesuvius and the old ridge of Mount Somma.

Not for the last time, those who lived within sight of Vesuvius had falsely come to believe that the fires of the Mouth of Hell had been extinguished.

11

THE NEW MOUNTAIN

FOR HUNDREDS OF YEARS during the Middle Ages and the early Renaissance, Vesuvius entered what Sir Charles Lyell, the nineteenth-century father of geology, called "a great pause." Vesuvius erupted in 1139, then was quiet again until 1306. During this period of repose, a vent opened north of Vesuvius resulting in an eruption of a volcano known as La Solfatara, or "Sulfur Earth," in 1198.

Vesuvius sits eight miles southeast of Naples, but it is not the area's only volcanic presence. The western suburb of Naples, Pozzuoli, is the center of the Phlegraean ("Fiery") Fields and the home of La Solfatara, which is still an active volcano. In 1538, several hundred years after the eruption of La Solfatara, the skin of the earth was suddenly pushed upward near Pozzuoli to form a new mountain, Monte Nuovo, where a tranquil village once stood near a lake. I had come to the Fiery Fields to see these two volcanic phenomena.

The crater of La Solfatara is a shallow dish approximately a mile in circumference in the very midst of the crowded city of Pozzuoli, its sides dotted with apartments built to the very edge of the volcanic cone. The presence of a live volcanic crater in a crowded suburb struck me as a disconcerting twentieth-century anomaly. The crater is easily accessible to any tourist for a few thousand lire, or a few American dollars. For a few thousand more lire you can camp along the edge and smell the sulfur wafting into your tent throughout the night.

I engaged fifty-five-year-old Angelo Rocco, a professional guide, who stared at me through mirrored sunglasses before agreeing to take me inside the volcano. Unlike Vesuvius, the crater of La Solfatara is easily entered. We began by walking down a gentle slope along a verdant pathway, then stepped easily into the crater, a desolate gray-white central plain. The stench of sulfurous smoke from several vents in the middle was nearly debilitating. We were encircled by low stone cliffs, their bare inner faces spouting curtains of frothy mist.

"Well, sir, here we are inside the crater of this volcano," Angelo intoned in a tour-guide litany. "There are twelve volcanoes all around Pozzuoli, but the only one active is this volcano here. This volcano is in communication with Vesuvius. This crater is larger than Vesuvius, but Vesuvius is deeper. . . ."

"When was the last eruption here?" I asked.

"The last eruption was in 1198, but we had a big scare in 1970."

We approached a circular area in the center, chained off, with numerous signs warning *"Pericolo"*—Danger. Ignoring the warning, Angelo lifted the chain and stepped under, then held it up for me. "Now the ground becomes more soft. Don't be scared. I'll go first. If I fall into the ground you go back."

We tramped along sandy soil mottled with hairline cracks and miniature fumaroles until we reached an inner circle, more securely chained off. Inside was a huge mudhole, thirty feet across, that percolated like a cauldron, venting the smell of rotten eggs. Two smaller mudholes lay behind it.

Angelo pointed to the most distant hole. "That one over there is very old," he said. "But here in front of us, ten years ago, we have nothing. One day there was a little hole in the ground, but every month it got bigger and bigger. Right now it is full of rainwater, but when it is dry this mud is more solid and sometimes it will explode outward.

"And that one"—he indicated the middle hole, about twelve feet wide—"opened about three months ago. Each day it is getting a little bigger. Before, we would walk right across there. Now we have to go around."

The spectacle of frothing sulfurous mud should be a perpetual reminder to the people of Pozzuoli that they live in a volcanic district, yet La Solfatara remains to them little more than a source of tourist revenues. As I stood there I could see Pozzuoli matrons in the distance hanging out their wash, oblivious to the foreigners strangely curious about the steaming holes in their ground.

Back outside the protective chain, Angelo pulled from his pocket a handful of broomstraws bounded by newspaper, then guided me toward a small series of fumaroles. "This phenomenon we call ionization," he said, as he set fire to the straws. "When I light this torch you will see, not in a few minutes but in a few seconds, more steam come out all over. That is a chain reaction."

He waved the torch above a fumarole, and steam billowed out with sudden violence all about us. A French tourist with a movie camera asked Angelo to repeat the trick, for he had missed it the first time.

"We can cook eggs, spaghetti, chicken here," Angelo said. "Saves on the gas bill."

We walked on toward the far side of the crater where a stone shack stood at the base of a sheltering cliff. "Sir, that little house there used to be an observatory. Beyond it, we have a little Vesuvius. We have dry sand at 150° Celsius, or 302° Fahrenheit."

Angelo then moved to the side and turned the stage over to a grizzled, emaciated man who awaited us behind the shack. "Approach, please," he beckoned to me. "Approach Little Vesuvius."

Little Vesuvius is extravagantly named, for it is a tiny steam jet encased in a small natural cave. The old man shoveled sand over the fumarole so that it bubbled upward. "Good morning, sir," he grinned. "Please now you see a small Vesuvius. Dry sand bubbling. Looks like water. That's from the steam. Open your hand, please." As he scooped hot sand into the palm of my hand, I made the suitable tourist exclamation of pain.

"You see now the Vesuvius in eruption miniature. And this is natural rocks from this volcano." He thrust a handful of stones at me, wrapped loosely in newspaper, then opened the packet and itemized them. "This is yellow sulfur crystals, natural color. Orange ammonia sulfide. This is lava black. And red mercury sulfide. You take for souvenir, sir. Something interesting for students, for boys in school. You take, please? This cost anything you wish for me, whatever you like."

I handed him a one-thousand-lire note and turned away from

Little Vesuvius to resume my tour with Angelo. "Well, sir, now we go to Purgatory and Hell," Angelo announced.

We trudged away from Little Vesuvius on a circular pathway that led around the crater edge to the far side and approached these two aptly named caves etched into the low cliffside, hot fumes emanating from their mouths. Suddenly a young woman emerged from the first cave, clad in the briefest of bikinis, a thin strand of red cloth covering only the lower half of her posterior, lumpy rolls of fat billowing out over the edge of the suit. A man followed her out of the cave, attired in a light-blue robe.

"She wants to lose weight," Angelo laughed. "Lots of people come here for that. The hot air in the caves is very good for the health." We approached the cave, which Angelo declared to be Purgatory. He gestured and I stepped inside, lowering my head slightly to avoid the overhanging ledge. I could see nothing, for my eyeglasses had immediately fogged in the 122° Fahrenheit heat.

"People stay in there for fifteen, twenty minutes. It's good for the skin, for asthma, for everything," Angelo assured me.

Directly next door was Hell. I thrust my hand into that cave as a timid test, but I quickly realized that I could not bear the heat. The temperature was a scalding 158° Fahrenheit. As I hesitated, the determined, bikini-clad woman pushed past me to enter.

Angelo and I continued on and soon completed our circuit of the crater, walking a quiet pathway guarded by cacti, myrtle and eucalyptus, whose mottled bark was decorated with lovers' initials. We passed the campground, restaurant and gift shop, after which I stepped out of the crater of a live volcano directly into the streets of Pozzuoli.

Once again, I was amazed at the audacity of the human species.

Pozzuoli is a market town. Each day farmers load bushels of fruit and other local produce into their dilapidated three-wheel trucks, payloads jammed in back, families compressed into the small cabs, and head for the busy marketplace on the Via Roma at the edge of the bay. Poorer farmers use donkey carts, while the poorest hitch themselves between the staves.

Across from the market is a tranquil public park, the guardian of a ghost from the past. It is now called the Temple of Serapis, but it was probably a market similar to the present one across the street, where first-century Roman citizens could bargain and barter.

In 1970 this relic of Roman culture provided a warning that the nearby crater, relegated only to eccentric foreigners, might soon threaten the town's existence. Measurements at the Temple of Serapis and at other locations in Pozzuoli revealed a dramatic change in the ground level, which rose more than three feet in a few months. Railway tracks became deformed; cracks appeared in the walls of apartment buildings in the vicinity of La Solfatara; a fresh, bubbling vent opened in the center of the volcanic crater. Even the most indifferent citizens of Pozzuoli realized that La Solfatara was agitated and might erupt for the first time in eight hundred years.

As soon as he learned of the unusual ground movement, Professor Giuseppe Imbo, former director of the observatory at Vesuvius, trucked a load of seismic equipment to the Pozzuoli area. Imbo's instruments recorded a flurry of mild activity in the ground under the Phlegraean Fields, but he could not be sure of its import, for the area had never been systematically monitored.

When Imbo reported his findings to worried local officials, they ordered an immediate evacuation. During the course of a single afternoon, with no prior warning, police forcibly moved six thousand people from their homes in the immediate vicinity of La Solfatara. As rumors of a possible volcanic eruption spread, another thirty thousand residents of Pozzuoli deserted their homes, overloading the roads in their panic. Carabinieri and soldiers were left to guard the near-empty suburb for weeks.

Gradually, as the seismic activity subsided and the ground fell back to its previous level, the people of Pozzuoli returned hesitantly to their homes. A decade has passed since that scare, and once more the neighbors of La Solfatara have forgotten that a volcano sleeps beside them.

The other spectacular phenomenon of the Fiery Fields—the New Mountain—seems paradoxical. Mountains, we have as-

sured ourselves, are the products of primeval geologic movements and do not rise from the earth in the midst of historic
times. Yet, in the Arco Felice section of Pozzuoli, there is just
such a mountain.

The mountain is approached from a side street, Via Virgil,
named after the famous poet who once lived in the area. The
narrow lane ends in a public park where a wide pathway of
crumbling stone leads up the side of Monte Nuovo. I trudged
four hundred feet up this path, with the Bay of Naples to my
back and the incessant noise of Pozzuoli's traffic below, to find
myself staring into the cone of yet another Neapolitan volcano.

In 1536 a plague of earthquakes descended upon Campania,
centered on the village of Tripergola, a convalescent resort
near Pozzuoli that was noted for its hot springs. The earthquakes continued intermittently for two years, and each time
the ground shook the anxious citizens gazed fearfully toward
nearby La Solfatara and the more distant Vesuvius.

On September 27, 1538, the earth shocks increased dramat-
ically in frequency. Throughout the day, the night, a second
day and a second night, the quakes continued. Fortunately, the
dramatic events of the week that followed were witnessed by
several people who left behind accounts of the extraordinary
birth of a mountain. One of these eyewitnesses was Marco
Antonio delli Falconi, whose letter to a friend was preserved
in a classic eighteenth-century volume, *Campi Phlegrai*, a description of Vesuvius and its environs written by Sir William
Hamilton, British envoy to the Court of Naples.

Delli Falconi counted twenty shocks on September 27 and
28. On the next day, Sunday, the faithful in local churches
sent their prayers heavenward with special intensity. While
the devout pleaded, a section of earth near Lake Lucrine at
Tripergola sank more than thirteen feet. Water, at first cold,
then lukewarm, oozed from the depression, and by noon the
land had begun to swell and rise.

Another contemporary observer of the phenomena was
Francesco del Nero, whose account of the event was discovered in 1848. Del Nero was standing in his garden near Tripergola when he heard an explosion as violent as a thunderclap
from the direction of Lake Lucrine. As blinding light electri-

fied the daytime sky, Del Nero overcame his fear and climbed to a nearby hill to watch the spectacle. He was astonished by the sight: A great gulf of fire stood where the lake had been a moment before. Flames moved skyward as earth and stones rose to a height he estimated at more than a mile and a half. Boulders, some as large as oxen, shot upward, then descended back upon the gulf.

Thick smoke, a strange mixture of sooty black and pure white, gushed upward, obscuring the view. As the pall spread out over Pozzuoli and Naples, thousands called out to San Gennaro for deliverance. The subterranean-based storm continued throughout the night, showering the countryside with ash, the constant roar reminding one observer of an artillery battle.

On Monday morning, September 30, flames burned through the cloud that shrouded Pozzuoli, whose alarmed residents were now fleeing to the countryside. They gathered food, including dead birds that had dropped from the sky and fish stranded on the expanding shoreline. All around them ashes and pebbles fell incessantly, impeding their flight.

The visitation continued, each explosion invoking still more pleas to the patron San Gennaro. It seemed that the saint heard; the explosions ceased during Monday night. Tuesday's morning sun revealed an unprecedented spectacle. Where two days earlier Lake Lucrine had been, there was now a mountain that stood 440 feet above the ground, its top a fuming volcanic cone. It was quickly named Monte Nuovo, or "New Mountain." Lake Lucrine was now a shallow pool off to one side, while the little village of Tripergola was simply obliterated.

An account by Pietro Giacomo di Toledo was also preserved in Hamilton's *Campi Phlegrai*. It continues the narrative of Monte Nuovo, a mountain that was soon to add more victims to Campania's volcanic death toll. The new mountain excited the curious, who joined Di Toledo in visiting it on Tuesday. Di Toledo climbed the slope of still-smoldering stones, awed by the size of the boulders that had been ejected out of the ground to form the hill. He worked his way to the top, where he estimated the crater rim to be a quarter mile in circumference. As he cautiously gazed over the edge, beneath him he could see a cavity nearly as deep as the mountain was high.

Far below was a red-orange cauldron in whose midst great stones boiled, proof that Monte Nuovo had not yet spent its energy.

Indeed, two nights later, on Thursday, October 3, 1538, the eruption rekindled. More smoke funneled skyward along with stones cast upward in such quantity that one observer, Marco Antonio delli Falconi, thought "they would cover the whole earth and sea." Then Monte Nuovo grew deceptively quiet. Smoke by day and fire by night signaled its existence, but the devastating discharge of boulders had ceased.

On Friday and Saturday the insatiably curious again ventured up to the new mountain, some as far as the summit. By Sunday, October 6, one week after it was born, Monte Nuovo was a prime attraction, drawing visitors from all over Campania to see the inexplicable phenomenon.

At ten o'clock that Sunday evening, while its slopes still held many visitors, Monte Nuovo suddenly reawoke with vigor. Smoke engulfed the sightseers, who rushed down in panic as volcanic vapors seared their lungs, stones pelted them and small cinders etched their flesh. Many lost their footing in the dark, sliding to their death in the loose stone. When the eruption subsided, twenty-four were dead, some of the bodies never located.

As abruptly as it rose, Monte Nuovo then settled into quietude amid the rolling geography of Campania, and has remained calm ever since. And what of Vesuvius during this period? Lyell wrote: "For nearly a century after the birth of Monte Nuovo, Vesuvius still continued in a state of tranquillity." But, like its deceptive posture many times in the past, stillness did not signal Vesuvius' death.

12

A WARNING FOR POSTERITY

DURING MY SEARCH through the Vesuvian countryside, I was particularly struck by the local people's ignorance of the history of the volcano that has so clearly shaped their life and land. Observers periodically remind residents of the danger, but the gentleness of the Campanian environment seems to anesthetize its citizens against the threat.

I had learned from Dr. Giuseppe Luongo of the Vesuvian Observatory that hundreds of years ago a plaque was erected somewhere in the village of Portici, warning its citizens of the evil of Vesuvius. Inscribed in Latin in 1632, the plaque has been all but forgotten by the town. One morning I decided to search for the plaque and study its bodeful message.

Portici is six miles west of Vesuvius, immediately north of the site of ancient Herculaneum on the Bay of Naples. My driver took me first to the university, where I spoke to the librarians, who were puzzled by my description of the plaque. They suggested that I question the village's fishermen, some of whom were expert in local oral history.

We drove along Corso Garibaldi, a busy main street, and turned down Via Emanuele Gianturco, edging toward the fishing docks. Moving along the edge of the bay, we stopped frequently to inquire of fishermen cleaning their boats. They admired our Fiat sedan, listened to our questions, but shook their heads in response.

"They say they never heard of such a plaque," my driver told me. Frustrated, we doubled back toward the business district and parked in a grassy piazza where children's amusement rides had been set up. The amiable octogenarian who ran the carousel prided himself on his knowledge of the city. He told us there were two plaques in Portici and gave us directions.

As we drove back along the Corso Garibaldi, my driver suddenly halted the car and pointed to a large bronze plaque imbedded into the stone of an office building. It was written in Italian, dated March 15, 1882. "It tells who built the building," he said with disappointment. "We look for the other."

Following the directions of the carousel man, we inched along the Corso Garibaldi, angering a line of impatient drivers behind us. "It should be here somewhere," the driver muttered.

"There!" I pointed to a marble slab ten feet above street level. It blended into the light gray stone of the building, making it difficult to see. It was at the intersection of Corso Garibaldi and Via Emanuele Gianturco, above the Cherie Perfume Shop. The plaque was composed of three rectangular marble panels eight feet wide and fifteen feet tall. The marble was cracked, especially at the seams of the three slabs, which someone had repaired with cement. Its message was etched in upper-case Latin.

An English translation of the now-forgotten plaque was made by the Earl of Orrery in 1751. To the unwitting citizens of Portici, the 350-year-old plaque warns:

> Posterity, posterity, this is your concern. . . .
> Be attentive.
> Twenty times, since the creation of the sun
> has Vesuvius blazed, never without a horrid
> destruction of those that hesitated to fly.
> This is a warning, that it may never
> seize you unapprized.
> The womb of this mountain is pregnant with
> bitumen, alum, iron, gold, silver, nitre,
> and fountains of water.
> Sooner or later it kindles, and when the sea
> rushes in, will give birth vent. . . .
> If you are wise, hear this speaking stone.
> Neglect your domestic concerns, neglect your

goods, and chattels, there is no delaying.
Fly.

—Anno Domini 1632, in the
reign of Philip IV,
Emmanuele Fonseca, Viceroy

I stood pensively on the sidewalk for some time, watching
the people of Portici scurry unsuspectingly beneath the old
forgotten plaque. Who was Emmanuele Fonseca, I wondered?
What had Vesuvius done in his day to warrant such an apoca-
lyptic warning?

By 1631, the year before the plaque was written, the throne
of Naples was occupied by Philip IV, King of Spain, King of
Naples, and King of Jerusalem. After centuries of control by
the Byzantines, the French Normans and the Germans, Naples
was now under the administration of King Philip's viceroy,
Emmanuele Fonseca, the author of the Portici plaque.

The condition of Vesuvius during this period was recorded
by an amateur naturalist, Magliocco. He descended into the
crater of Vesuvius in 1619 and found a massive rock at its
center. Examining the fissures around its base, he discovered
that this one huge boulder blocked the vent of Vesuvius. Only
an immense explosion could dislodge it.

That force, in the form of earthquakes, struck Vesuvius in
the second half of 1631. Some citizens noticed the characteristic precursors of volcanic action: The springs and wells dried
up and the animal population grew confused and subdued.
Some believe that these natural signs are mere folklore, but
scientists now think that just before earthquakes and volcanic
eruptions, the subterranean earth faults fracture even more,
causing the water table to drop and wells to dry up.

Animal sensitivity to earthquakes and volcanoes has been
observed throughout the world as well, but it is less well
understood. Some scientists feel that it is due to acute animal
responsiveness to faint seismic vibrations, or to changes in the
localized magnetic field, forces to which humans are apparently insensitive.

But there were a few signs that were decipherable to humans. Bellowing sounds emanated from the interior of Vesuvius. Concerned residents decided to climb the mountain and were astonished to learn that the crater, only a hollow dish months before, was now filled with an amalgam of solid and liquid rock. They returned home to warn their neighbors of the activity, but some, including the residents of Torre del Greco, a bay village four miles west of Vesuvius, expressed indifference.

A more pressing concern overshadowed the fear of Vesuvius. The Black Death, the plague of 1631, was now epidemic throughout the Vesuvian countryside. The plague produced symptoms of high fever, nausea, violent headache, and either the inflamed lymph nodes of the bubonic form or the bloody coughing spasms of the pneumonic variety. Ironically, the fear of these horrors indirectly led to more deaths from Vesuvius than were caused by the plague itself.

On the morning of Wednesday, December 16, 1631, Vesuvius burst open with a deafening explosion. The familiar manifestations of an eruption—an ash cloud, lightning, earth spasms and volcanic bombs—terrorized the countryside. An observer, Antonio Bulifon, reported that one huge boulder had landed twelve miles away in the town of Nola, destroying the house of the Marquis of Lauro.

More than forty thousand refugees fled northward away from Vesuvius, but were denied entrance to towns along the Bay of Naples by Campanians who feared they were carrying the Black Death with them. Turned away from the smaller towns, the refugees converged upon the locked gates of Naples. Viceroy Fonseca did not want to admit the mob, but he could not ignore their desperation. Seeing an encroaching black cloud raining ash and hot cinders not far behind them, Fonseca reluctantly ordered the gates of Naples unlocked.

All of Naples turned to San Gennaro for deliverance, but the frightened archbishop refused to carry the holy vial of the saint's blood to the city limits where it was traditionally raised in the direction of Vesuvius. Incensed at the archbishop's reluctance, the crowd burned the gates of his palace.

In the bayside village of Torre del Greco, official calm contrasted with the panic that now gripped most of Campania. Fearing the Black Death more than the volcano, the mayor instructed his citizens to remain within the village walls, a decision that was to make Torre del Greco the Pompeii of its day.

Throughout Wednesday night the citizens of Torre del Greco stayed in their homes praying for deliverance, much as the Pompeiians had done in A.D. 79. The Roman gods had been exchanged for a Christian deity, but Vesuvius was as indifferent as ever.

The next day Vesuvius ruptured on its flanks instead of through the crater. A fountain of water-saturated lava, lighter and faster moving than the conventional form, poured out from two fissures on the southern slope. This hot material, described by some as boiling water mingled with loose ash, then flowed rapidly down the mountainside, splitting into several divergent streams.

The largest of the west streams headed toward Torre del Greco, where the people realized their peril too late. Moving forward with greater velocity than ordinary lava, the stream was already at the village walls when the mayor finally ordered an evacuation. The villagers were running through the streets when the hot flood cascaded over the walls and inundated the city with wet fire. Homes, trees, domestic animals and thousands of human victims were engulfed in the boiling deluge, which drove their bodies through the descending streets down into the Bay of Naples.

Those who returned to Torre del Greco found a silent city buried under a crusted layer of steaming lava. Charred remains of human and animal flesh were scattered through the debris. Pockets of gas, trapped within the cooling rock, puffed out explosively. Though the loss of life was greatest among those who tarried at Torre del Greco, where thousands were boiled alive, the physical devastation was as great in other coastal towns, particularly in Torre dell' Annunziata and Portici. Estimates of the death toll throughout Campania reached as high as eighteen thousand, making the 1631 eruption more lethal than the one that had destroyed Pompeii.

Vesuvius, too, had suffered. The uppermost portions of the volcano were truncated, decreasing the height of the cone by more than five hundred feet. The internal changes were less obvious but more ominous; in 1631 Vesuvius had entered a new geological era. Previously it had erupted after lengthy intervals of hundreds or thousands of years, during which time residents insisted that the volcano was extinct. But now Vesuvius would rarely lapse into repose.

After viewing the destruction of the countryside, Viceroy Emmanuele Fonseca chiseled his warning about Vesuvius into marble as an immutable message to posterity. That plaque still stands in Portici at the corner of Corso Garibaldi and Via Emanuele Gianturco, where every day thousands of Campanians unknowingly pass by the silent warning.

Some stop in at the Cherie Perfume Shop below the plaque; others study the lurid movie posters across the street. But no one pauses to consider the passionate advice of Emmanuele Fonseca, written 350 years ago in the universal Latin tongue: "Fly!"

13

THE LOST CITIES

VESUVIUS HAD BURIED POMPEII, Herculaneum and several smaller cities with such dispatch that much of their ancient glory was preserved intact beneath ash and mud. But by the beginning of the eighteenth century only a few scholars knew these Roman towns had ever existed, and even they were unaware of the locations of the fabled ruins. The eroding processes of nature and the indifference of medieval societies to history had erased almost every trace of what had become the lost Roman cities.

The story of their discovery in the eighteenth century is an uncommon union of serendipity and misfortune, care and error. The chronicle begins at the villa in Portici built by Emanuel Moritz von Lotheringia, the Austrian Prince d'Elboeuf.

I decided to find the villa, if it still existed. Returning to the university library in Portici, I asked about the Villa d'Elboeuf. One librarian offered me a faded volume of villas with sketches of the most prominent ones. Fortunately, it included the object of my search.

My driver was able to locate the villa north of the town's fishing wharf. As we drove up to the building, I could see that the magnificent external lines had been preserved. There was one significant internal change: It was now an apartment house for middle-income families.

One tenant was drying her laundry on a first-floor terrace as her daughter played at her feet. I introduced myself to the young housewife, Giovanna Simeone, and asked if this was a good building in which to live. She assured me that it was one of the best in Portici for the price. When I explained that her apartment was built in 1711 by an Austrian prince upon a slab of lava from the 1631 eruption that had destroyed almost all of Portici, Giovanna was astounded. As we walked along a sea-washed promenade I told her that her home, once a magnificent estate, had played a central role in the story of Vesuvius, particularly in the discovery of the lost cities.

It is not clear at what point the locations of Pompeii and Herculaneum were lost, but by the seventeenth century only vague speculations circulated in the scholarly world. Conventional theory held that a hill called Civita (derived from the Latin word for "state"), located about six miles south of Vesuvius, was the site of an ancient settlement. Most believed that Stabiae lay buried there, but no one could find the exact site.

In the early 1700s, Austria, under the leadership of Prince Eugene of Savoy, had conquered the kingdom of Naples. The Austrians were disliked, but one of the ruling clique who gained acceptance in Neapolitan society was Prince d'Elboeuf, a distant cousin of Prince Eugene. D'Elboeuf was given command of the Austrian guard in Naples, a position he enhanced by hosting lavish banquets from his rented city palazzo. Within a year he announced his engagement to a Neapolitan princess, Salsa.

D'Elboeuf was determined to create a royal villa for his bride, and in 1711, he purchased a parcel of land, west of Vesuvius, from the monastery of San Petro d'Alcantara. The prince imported a Frenchman who fashioned a brilliant porcelain material from crushed stone and marble, from which he constructed d'Elboeuf's country palace, the building I had located in modern Portici.

The prince then contacted a *marmoraro*, a tradesman peculiar to Italy. It was relatively common for a landowner to dig up fragments of ancient marble, which he sold to a marmoraro who, in turn, resold them to craftsmen who made the stone into decorative fountains or statues of saints. It was such a marmoraro who first showed the prince fragments of a special yellow marble that was highly prized in Roman times. When d'Elboeuf realized that these pieces were clearly portions of

ancient pillars, he persuaded the marmoraro to take him to
the source.

An elegant procession descended upon the peasant cottage
of Giovanni Nocerino in Resina, immediately south of Portici.
Nocerino explained that his well had begun to dry up and that
he was digging it lower when he encountered the fragments.
He also exhibited several other pieces, which the prince immediately purchased. Returning to Portici, d'Elboeuf and his
Neapolitan architect, Giuseppe Stendardo, studied the pieces.
When Stendardo concluded that an ancient classical building
lay under the peasant's fields, the prince quickly bought Nocerino's land.

Workmen descended to the base of the well and tunneled
horizontally in every direction. Within days they discovered a
vault containing a marble statue of Hercules. In the same vault
workmen found the statue of a woman minus an arm and a
foot, which they took to be Cleopatra, and a fifteen-foot-long
marble slab.

When cleaned of centuries of dirt, the marble slab revealed
foot-high metallic Latin letters embedded in its surface, its
inscription bearing the name of Appius Pulcher, son of Gaius.
Some days later three beautiful female statues were found, a
mother and two daughters, which captivated d'Elboeuf with
their classical allure.

D'Elboeuf decided to give the three female statues to his
kinsman, Prince Eugene of Savoy. Since it was illegal to take
classical art out of Italy without the Pope's permission,
d'Elboeuf arranged to smuggle the statues out by sea to Tri-
este, then to Prince Eugene in Vienna. The Austrian prince
put the statues on public display, and they became widely
known throughout Europe as the Vestal Virgins.

News of the smuggled treasures reached Cardinal Quirini,
the papal librarian, who complained to the Austrian viceroy in
Naples, who, in turn, harangued d'Elboeuf. The prince gradually abandoned his work, for despite the attention focused on
his finds, he was still unsure of their ultimate meaning.

After he was transferred to France, d'Elboeuf sold the villa
and its classical contents, but the new owners were not inter-
ested in the excavation. Fortunately, the palazzo eventually

fell into the hands of a royal family whose acquisitive and cultural interests were to ensure that the search for the lost cities would continue.

In 1734, eighteen-year-old Charles of Bourbon assumed the thrones of Naples and Sicily. Since Naples offered little choice gaming land, Charles bought the palazzo in Portici built by the Prince d'Elboeuf. The king was gratified by the unexpected bonus, the store of art treasures retrieved from some unknown classical source.

History is at times shaped from apparently disconnected parts that suddenly, and fortuitously, blend. A remarkable series of events bridging Vienna, Dresden and Naples was to bring Vesuvius to world attention by resolving the mystery of the lost cities. D'Elboeuf had stumbled upon significant evidence, but had failed to understand its implications. In the 1730s, chance and inspiration of a young royal bride would provide the key.

The chain of circumstance began with the death of Prince Eugene of Savoy in 1736. His closest survivor was his niece, Anna Victoria, who proved to be a mercenary heiress. As the chief of the Imperial Austrian Archives wrote: "With a greed that was truly disgusting, she set about realizing as speedily as possible all that her husband had left. Not a thing was spared, everything was ruthlessly turned into money."

Anna Victoria even sold the three Vestal Virgins to King Augustus III of Poland, who dispatched them to his palace in Dresden where they were admired by his daughter, Maria Amalia Christine. In 1738 Maria became Queen Maria of the Kingdoms of Naples and Sicily. On her first visit to the villa at Portici, she marveled at the statues unearthed by d'Elboeuf's crew. Dreaming of possessing her own Vestal Virgins, she persuaded her new husband to resume the search abandoned a quarter of a century before.

Charles engaged a Spanish engineer, Rocco Gioacchino de Alcubierre, who began digging at the well site in 1738. Discoveries came quickly: fragments of two huge bronze horses, a pair of giant busts of Roman aristocrats hewn from marble, brick pillars, another marble statue. Alcubierre's crew also uncovered a long stairway that seemed to be part of the stage of a theater. But what theater, in what ancient city, Alcubierre did not know.

On December 11, the diggers unearthed a plaque inscribed in Latin. Lucius Annius Mammianus Rufus, it declared, has financed the construction of this building, the "Theatrum Herculanensum." The ancient lost city of Herculaneum, destroyed by an earthslide of Vesuvian mud in A.D. 79, had finally been discovered.

These early results must be considered in context. It was 1738, a time when archaeology was almost nonexistent as a discipline. Knowledge was not the goal; treasure was. The work was further hampered because Charles insisted that the project be kept secret. He hoped to make Naples as celebrated an artistic center as Florence and sought to amass a large enough collection before announcing his extraordinary finds to the world.

Discoveries multiplied as Alcubierre's diggers haphazardly enlarged their channels, sometimes smashing through walls and destroying ancient frescoes. Bits of a chariot and bronze racing horses were found. A large lead statue, covered in bronze, thought to be that of the Emperor Titus, proved too heavy to remove.

Most of the art objects were fragmentary, crushed to bits by Vesuvian mud. Charles then hired Joseph Canart, a sculptor, to restore the treasures, but he too proved destructive, melting priceless metal fragments to strike new statues for the king. Frescoes that survived the frantic dig were covered with a protective veneer, but when that flaked off, the paintings were lost forever. An inscription written in large metallic letters was thrown, letter after letter, into a basket before anyone thought of recording the Latin text. The dig was a warren of narrow passages where the crew labored under the threat of cave-ins. Once treasure was removed from a tunnel, it was filled in before new channels were dug, reburying the ancient homes and shops.

Despite King Charles' passion for secrecy, he could not keep the news from filtering out. In 1740, the youthful enthusiasm of one influential visitor was to focus world attention on the discovery. He was Horace Walpole, the twenty-three-year-old son of the British Prime Minister, Sir Robert Walpole.

Fascinated by Herculaneum, young Walpole wrote to a friend:

> We ... have seen something today that I am sure you never read of. Have you ever heard of a subterranean town? A whole Roman town with all its edifices remaining underground? You remember in Titus' time there were several cities destroyed by an eruption of Vesuvius, attended with an earthquake. Well, this was one of them, not very considerable, and then called Herculaneum. Above it has been built Portici, about three miles from Naples, where the king has a villa. This underground city is perhaps one of the noblest curiosities that ever has been discovered. ... But I believe there is no judicious choice made of directors. There is nothing of the kind known in the world; I mean a Roman city entire of that age, and that has not been corrupted with modern repairs.

Walpole's letter arrived in England at a propitious time, when classical interest was heightening and groups such as the Society of the Dilettanti had been formed to promote the study of antiquity.

In Naples, scholars urged King Charles to make his discoveries accessible to the educated public. The young king realized that Alcubierre was incompetent at archaeology; he needed someone to present the Roman excavations to the world in a systematic form. Unfortunately, Charles commissioned the cousin of a minister, Monsignor Ottavio Antonio Bayardi, to prepare a public exhibition of the finds. Citing asthma as an excuse, the old scholar refused to inspect the tunnels at Herculaneum and retreated to his classical library to fashion a lengthy introduction to an exhibit catalog.

By 1745 the work seemed to be yielding more aggravation than treasure, and King Charles suspended the excavations at Herculaneum. As that work stopped, speculation increased about the hill called Civita, six miles south of Vesuvius. Several Neapolitan scholars proclaimed it to be the site of Pompeii, but Alcubierre insisted Stabiae lay there. Shortly after King Charles ordered excavations to begin in 1748, a worker's spade unearthed human bones, then an entire skeleton. It was that of a man fleeing Vesuvius at the moment of his death,

Roman coins from the reigns of Nero and Vespasian strewn about him.

By November work had shifted to a large oval depression where rows of seats had been unearthed. Alcubierre proclaimed it the Stabiaen Theatre. Some time later an ancient villa was uncovered, which Alcubierre mistakenly labeled as Cicero's. After removing its statues and frescoes, he re-covered the villa with soil. Alcubierre had found relatively little treasure for his patron. The work at Civita also gradually ceased, the secret of its identity still buried.

Charles then decided to renew the excavations at Herculaneum with the help of a young Swiss architect, Karl Weber, whom he employed to assist Alcubierre. With this appointment began a tense professional conflict between the interests of haphazard treasure hunting and true archaeological search. Alcubierre's hunt for plunder remained dominant, but Weber disregarded many orders and began to draw intricate plans of the excavated buildings before they could be reburied and lost forever.

Alcubierre's indifference to archaeological research eventually created an error at Herculaneum of such magnitude that even modern techniques have been unable to rectify it. In 1750, near Resina, workers discovered a lavish ancient villa whose great peristyle was surrounded by sixty-four pillars. Inside the home was a magnificent oblong bath and galleries of fine classical art. Statuary was abundant: One bronze group included a comical drunken faun, nubile dancing girls and two Greek youths poised to wrestle one another. Forty-seven lifelike busts were carved in marble. The excavators gradually uncovered expansive living rooms, verandas and courtyards.

It was October 19, 1752, when the workers' spades penetrated a small room at the far end of this villa. In the center of the room was a free-standing set of shelves on which were stored strange cylindrical objects that resembled charcoal logs. Some crumbled to dust at the workers' touch, but Alcubierre's crew became more cautious when one of the men noticed writing on a charred cylinder.

Alcubierre summoned Camillo Paderni, curator of the collection at the Portici palace, who studied the puzzling blackened rolls and declared them to be specimens of ancient papyri. The lost writings of classical scholars were in Paderni's grasp. He removed nearly two thousand full rolls and fragments from the library and stored them at Portici until a safe method of unrolling them could be devised.

In the wake of this discovery came Alcubierre's historic archaeological blunder. Once the artistic treasures and books were removed, he reburied the estate. The detailed plans of the villa, drawn by Alcubierre's assistant, Karl Weber, remain, but the location of the Villa of the Papyri has been lost forever.

The scholarly world was now impatient, awaiting an official report of the finds at Herculaneum. By 1752, after a decade of labor, Monsignor Ottavio Antonio Bayardi had written 2,677 pages of introductory material to the Herculaneum catalog without describing a single find. The Marchese Caracciolo complained: "So far Mr. Bayardi has taken pleasure in burying the ancient world of Herculaneum beneath a much denser veil than that spread over it by the lava."

Spurred by an exasperated King Charles, Bayardi three years later issued a catalog with descriptions of more than twenty-five hundred objects unearthed from Herculaneum. This fascinating, if belated, encyclopedia offered an unprecedented insight into the life and art of the Roman Empire and was a major stimulus for the birth of the neoclassical movement in art and architecture.

The excavations began to exert a magnetic influence on the growing class of the upper bourgeoisie for whom the classical ruins were a symbol of culture. In the decades that followed, the ruins affected virtually every Western art including dance, architecture and painting, even to the design of fabrics and Wedgwood china, all of which incorporated the newly rediscovered Roman themes.

When Ferdinand VI of Spain died in 1759, Charles returned to Madrid and the scepter of Naples passed to twelve-year-old Ferdinand IV, a monarch who was considered ignorant and was unconcerned with the ruins. Fortunately, the excavations had a champion in Prime Minister Bernardo Tanucci, who continued the work.

By this time, it was becoming apparent that the diggers at Civita were uncovering an entire town, including a city gate with a large archway for cart traffic, flanked by two smaller pedestrian entrances. North of this gate the workers found a large inn and five human skeletons along with such household articles as bottles, pots and pans, and keys. The next find proved to be a large tomb, with an epitaph to a priestess named Mamia. It was initially believed that Tanucci's crew had discovered Stabiae, where Pliny the Elder had died.

Then on August 16, 1763, a propitious discovery cleared the mystery of Civita. A white marble statue was unearthed, accompanied by an inscription: "In the name of the Emperor and Caesar Vespasian Augustus, the tribune T. Svedius Clemens has restored . . . to the public possession of the Pompeiians, those places which belonged to them and had been taken into private possession."

The legendary lost city of Pompeii had been found.

14

THE LORD OF VESUVIUS

NOT LONG AFTER the discovery of Herculaneum and Pompeii in the mid–eighteenth century, one particularly perceptive individual entered the story of Vesuvius. If there is a protagonist in this drama other than the volcano itself, it is a British statesman whose infatuation with the mountain gave the world the first comprehensive eyewitness reports of an eruption in progress.

He took a provincial volcano whose ancient Roman victims were only now being uncovered, and made it world famous as the subject of a scientific and humanistic dialogue. He was Sir William Hamilton, British envoy to the court of Naples, and, to posterity, the Lord of Vesuvius.

Hamilton first became fascinated by the fiery mountain, so foreign to his quiet English soil, on Good Friday, March 28, 1766, when he observed the birth of the eruption from his villa in Portici, located directly in the path of the approaching lava. It was the beginning of a love affair between the slender, foppish aristocrat and the great volcano.

The affair would far transcend science, for Hamilton saw in the volcano a diabolical beauty to which he was irresistibly drawn. He later found himself in a similar situation, eager to cast off the conventions of his genteel upbringing, when he began an affair with another unconventional love, the famous Lady Emma Hamilton, who later became the mistress of British naval hero Lord Horatio Nelson.

Hamilton was born in Scotland on December 13, 1730, the son of Lord Archibald Hamilton, a former governor of Jamaica. At age sixteen, William embarked upon a military career, but was able to forsake the army eleven years later when he married a Welsh heiress. A Renaissance man who dreamed of the classical life, Hamilton was inspired by news of the discoveries of Pompeii and Herculaneum and traveled to Naples at the age of thirty-three, where he was soon appointed British ambassador to the court of His Sicilian Majesty, Ferdinand IV.

With little official business to transact, Hamilton turned to scientific pursuits, particularly those involving the historic trio of Vesuvius, Pompeii and Herculaneum. He and his Welsh wife took up residence at the Villa Angelica to be near the excavation. Living only six miles west of the summit, he became a habitual, even addicted, Vesuvius watcher.

The eruption that began on Good Friday of 1766 proved to be a mild one, and by Easter Sunday Hamilton felt secure enough to spend Monday night upon the slopes of Vesuvius with his friend Frederick Hervey. He marveled at his first sight of volcanic bombs—so hot, he said, that they were transparent. He watched, absorbed, as they jettisoned hundreds of feet into the air, then crashed back explosively into the crater.

Hamilton sent a report of the event to the Royal Society of London, which published it in their journal, *Philosophical Transactions*. The high praise it received encouraged Hamilton to keep a record of the volcano's activity, and over the next thirty years, he would become the world's major source of information about Vesuvius. Through the volcano, he was to build a scientific reputation that would transcend his political fame and provide a shield against the personal notoriety he would later suffer.

Hamilton studied every idiosyncracy of the volcano, quickly dispatching the news to London. Eruptions were not the only activity that fascinated him. On two occasions he noticed that mofettes, unexplained pockets of cold carbon dioxide, had issued silently from vents on the lower slopes of Vesuvius and spread into the neighboring towns. Hamilton recalled that when a servant of the king opened the door of the royal chapel at Portici, he walked into a mofette and suffocated to death. In the second incident, a royal hunting dog mysteriously collapsed. A boy who ran to aid the animal was also overcome, but both were pulled into the fresh air and safety.

To his Fellows at the Royal Society, he confided his growing obsession with Vesuvius:

> I cannot have a greater pleasure than to employ my leisure hours in what may be of some little use to mankind, and my lot has carried me into a country which affords me an ample field for observations. . . . The subject of volcanoes is so favourite a one to me, that it has led me on I know not how.

Hamilton climbed Vesuvius scores of times. In May 1779, accompanied by a local guide and a Mr. Bowdler of Bath, England, Hamilton was drawn to its slopes during an eruption. On an evening illuminated by the orange glow of molten rock, they approached a lava stream fifty feet wide, careful to remain upwind to avoid being overcome by smoke.

Suddenly the wind changed, sending scalding sulfurous smoke into their faces, nearly asphyxiating all three men. The blinding smoke swirled all about them, cutting off their escape. The Englishmen watched in astonishment as their guide sprinted toward the lava stream hoping to reach clean air on the other side. They stood transfixed as the guide walked across the molten rock, convinced that he would sink into the burning river.

When the Englishmen saw that he had gained the far side safely, they followed quickly, heat searing their expensive boots. Surprisingly, the strong crust of the lava supported their weight as long as they maintained forward motion. In moments they had crossed the fifty-foot gauntlet and were once again upwind, coughing off the fumes and inspecting their scorched boots. Hamilton's curiosity was finally sated, and he and his companions retreated downslope.

Vesuvius was quiet for months, until August 7, 1779, when an explosion fractured windows and walls in Portici, driving its inhabitants into the streets. Looking to Vesuvius, they saw a fountain of fire rising from the central crater, in apparent slow motion, three times larger than the mountain itself. Pushed slightly off center by wind currents, the hot pyroclastic material arched downward, then headed inexorably toward the village of Ottaviano.

Flight was impossible: The villagers took refuge in their homes or in the churches. Those who attempted to run were driven back as the bombs, some as large as eight feet in diameter, cascaded to the ground, turning everything combustible to tinder.

After days of agitation, Vesuvius settled once more into repose. Ottaviano was desolated, with four feet of rubble now blocking the narrow streets. Hamilton visited the town a few days later and was impressed by the resolve of the villagers who were already piling volcanic debris into orderly mounds and rebuilding their homes.

Hamilton pondered both the vulnerability and the tenacity of the human species. At the end of a cycle of destruction, life had begun anew, a lesson he was to employ over the next few years. In 1782, Hamilton's wife died, leaving him independently wealthy but painfully lonely. Like the villagers of Ottaviano, he had to find a way to rebuild.

In 1783, Hamilton's nephew, Charles Grenville, arrived in Naples for a visit, accompanied by his eighteen-year-old mistress, Emma Lyon. Emma, the daughter of a Cheshire blacksmith, had lived with Grenville for the past two years while he financed her singing, dancing and acting lessons. Hamilton immediately saw in the vivacious beauty a reflection of the idealized classical woman through whom he could revitalize his life. He took his nephew on a tour of Vesuvius, but it was Emma who monopolized his thoughts.

Two years later, when Grenville wrote Hamilton from England requesting financial aid to rescue him from bankruptcy, Hamilton offered to help if his nephew would cede his mistress. Grenville agreed to the trade, but Emma resented the arrangement, even though she finally acquiesced. Once in Naples, she became attracted to the scholarly, balding Hamilton and to his rising fame and fortune. The British ambassador, convinced that life's conventions were meaningless, decided to live openly with Emma.

Hamilton, the classicist, often dressed Emma in Grecian garb. For the entertainment of his guests, he placed Emma inside a large gilt frame in which she struck *poses plastiques,* which received first local, then international, attention. German poet Johann Wolfgang von Goethe, a dinner guest of

Hamilton and his Lady Emma, was one of those entranced by her performance.

He later wrote:

> Sir William Hamilton, who is still living here as English ambassador, has now, after many years of devotion to the arts and the study of nature, found the acme of these delights in the person of an English girl of twenty with a beautiful face and a perfect figure. He has had a Greek costume made for her which becomes her extremely. Dressed in this, she lets down her hair and, with a few shawls, gives so much variety to her poses, gesture, expressions, etc., that the spectator can hardly believe his eyes. . . . This much is certain: as a performance it's like nothing you ever saw before in your life.

Though the arrangement between the British ambassador and his lady never lost its scandalous taint, Emma became a favorite of Neapolitan society, particularly of Queen Carolina, and she regularly brought Hamilton news of Ferdinand's court. Twenty-eight years after he first came to Naples, Sir William Hamilton, now 60, declared that he did not care "a pin for the world," and married his twenty-six-year-old mistress, Emma Lyon, during a visit to England in September 1791.

Upon his return to Naples there was considerable gossip that Hamilton had sold his illegal private collection of relics from Herculaneum and Pompeii to the British Museum for eighty-four hundred pounds in order to finance Emma's lavish tastes. But to Hamilton, fortune was secondary; life itself was the reward. In a note to Emma he elaborated on his philosophy: "My study of antiquities has kept me in constant thought of the perpetual fluctuation of everything. The whole art is, really, to live all the *days* of our life; and not, with anxious care, disturb the sweetest hours that life affords."

Emma was already a confidante of Queen Carolina, but as Lady Hamilton she was now more socially acceptable to all the courtiers. It was an important personal and political alliance, for Naples and Britain were growing more dependent upon one another, particularly in face of the new threat to monarchy emanating from revolutionary Paris. One of the threatened was Marie Antoinette, Queen of France and the sister of Carolina. In January 1793, news reached Naples that King Louis XVI had been guillotined. When the new government of revolutionary France declared war on Britain, Hamilton and Lady Emma became central figures in the court of Naples, which now sought to align itself closely with the English.

To demonstrate support for their new Neapolitan allies, the British sent Admiral Horatio Nelson to Naples, where he arrived on September 11, 1793, aboard the *Agamemnon*. The Hamiltons welcomed the naval hero to their villa, beginning an eccentric friendship that would eventually scandalize all Europe.

By early June 1794, a thick vapor of unknown origin appeared below the summit of Vesuvius, causing both the sun and the moon to appear with an unusual reddish cast. A man and two boys working in a vineyard upslope from Torre del Greco suddenly noticed smoke bursting from the ground. A week later, underground rumblings were heard near Resina.

On Sunday, June 15, 1794, just after ten P.M., Naples was shaken by a brief earthquake. Moments later, fifteen fountains of pyroclastic material exploded from various fissures along the western fault system of Vesuvius. The mammoth stream of lava at first threatened Resina, then took an abrupt turn to the south and veered toward Torre del Greco. Unlike their ancestors who tarried in 1631, its eighteen thousand residents quickly evacuated the town. The lava moved in rapidly behind them, over the walls of Torre del Greco, burning through the center of town. It then slid 626 feet into the bay where the hot mass exploded violently before settling into place as a twelve-foot-high promontory. Fifteen people, mostly aged and disabled, died.

The next morning Hamilton went to Torre del Greco by boat to view the devastation, but he could not move closer than one hundred yards from the shore. The water of the bay was still scalding hot; white smoke hissed from the new lava shelf extending into the bay. Occasionally portions of the lava surface peeled off, revealing a red-hot inner core. Hamilton could only observe the phenomenon for a few minutes, for his small craft had sprung leaks where the hot sea water had melted the pitch on the bottom of the boat. He hurriedly beached the boat off to one side of town.

On land, Hamilton walked to the edge of Torre del Greco, climbing to a rooftop vantage point at the edge of the lava. Timbers still smoldered in a few houses. The lava averaged twelve feet in depth, but had massed forty feet high in some areas. The town church was engulfed, leaving only the bell tower visible.

A fortnight later, Hamilton, for the sixty-eighth time, climbed Vesuvius with his guide, Bartholeo Pumo. They walked downslope the full five-mile length of the lava flow to Torre del Greco, where they found the villagers digging out. Hamilton was once again cheered at the optimistic nature of man.

Reporting to the Royal Society, he said:

The late sufferers at Torre del Greco, though his Sicilian Majesty offered them a more secure spot to rebuild their town on, are obstinately employed in rebuilding it on the late and still smoking lava that covers their former habitations; and there does not appear to be any situation more exposed to the numerous dangers that must attend the neighbourhood of an active volcano than that of Torre del Greco. It was totally destroyed in 1631; and in the year 1737, a dreadful lava ran within a few yards of one of the gates of the town, and now over the middle of it; yet such is the attachment of the inhabitants to their native spot, though attended with such imminent danger, that of 18,000 not one gave his vote to abandon it. . . .

This was to be Hamilton's last major report on his beloved volcano, for political events soon overtook him. By 1798, Napoleon's General Louis-Alexandre Berthier had captured the Eternal City and driven out the Pope. Though Hamilton thought Ferdinand an inept leader, he encouraged the Neapolitan king to restore papal authority in Rome. Admiral Horatio Nelson, who had returned to help Naples after his victories over the French in Egypt, joined Hamilton in pressing this adventure upon the hapless Neapolitan king. Ferdinand did march on Rome, but his army was routed.

The defeat brought about the end of Hamilton's affair with

Vesuvius. When Ferdinand decided to flee to Sicily, Hamilton and Lady Emma joined the royal couple aboard Nelson's flagship. With Naples lost to Napoleon, Hamilton was soon recalled to Britain from Sicily.

It was during this inglorious return that the scandalous friendship between Hamilton, Emma and the flamboyant Nelson began its course. While traveling overland, Emma became Nelson's mistress, apparently with the concurrence of her aging husband. Emma bore Nelson a son on January 30, 1801, yet Hamilton's love for her remained fast. His life in Naples, his association with Vesuvius, was ended. Emma was all he had.

Sir William Hamilton, British ambassador to Naples, Fellow of the Royal Society of London, died on April 6, 1803, at the age of seventy-two, leaving Emma an annual stipend of eight hundred pounds and his household furniture.

Nelson's wife left him after learning of his affair with Lady Hamilton. After Hamilton's death, Nelson took Emma to live with him at his Merton estate, departing on September 13, 1805, for his climactic victory at the Battle of Trafalgar, where he defeated the French fleet but was fatally wounded. He left Emma the Merton estate and an annual income of five hundred pounds. But Lady Emma Hamilton, widowed by both her husband and her lover, continued her profligate life. In 1813 she was thrown into debtor's prison. She died on January 15, 1815, at the age of fifty.

It would be a disservice to dismiss Hamilton's detailed studies of Vesuvius as a mere chronicle of destruction. Hamilton was a devoted admirer of nature's grace, which he saw at its fullest in both Emma and in the volcano. On May 1, 1776, he wrote a letter to Sir John Pringle, president of the Royal Society of London, in which he described Vesuvius as a force for good as well as evil, as an agent of not only "calamity," but beauty itself.

Said Hamilton:

There is no doubt, but that the neighbourhood of an active volcano must suffer from time to time the most dire calamities, the natural attendants of earthquakes, and eruptions. . . . The Campania Felix, that delicious and fertile spot, Misenum, Baia, Pozzuoli, the delight of many emperors, and Roman chiefs, whose beauties have been celebrated by so many poets . . . and the delightful situation of Naples itself, all have been produced, and owe their beauty, and variety of their scenery to such seeming destruction.

Like few others, Sir William Hamilton, the Lord of Vesuvius, recognized the intricacy of nature's scheme disguised amid the flames of the volcano.

15

THE GRAND TOUR

IN THE EIGHTEENTH AND NINETEENTH CENTURIES, no fashionable young man could call himself properly educated unless he had undertaken an obligatory Grand Tour of Europe. Such a journey often took a year or more to accomplish as the emerging gentleman visited the great cities of the continent: Amsterdam, Brussels, Paris, Vienna, Berlin, Munich, Dresden, Athens. Northern and central Italy, particularly the cities of Venice, Florence, and Rome, were supremely important in this fashionable scheme.

Soon after the discovery of the lost cities, Pompeii, Herculaneum and Vesuvius became a trio of prime destinations on the Grand Tour. Neapolitans discovered the profitable side of their new popularity, constructing grand hotels to accommodate the influx. Carriages carried the guests past Portici to Herculaneum and beyond to Pompeii. Professional guides shepherded parties of visitors to Vesuvius, for the ancient Roman cities were most meaningful after a journey to the source of their destruction.

Into this milieu, the eighteenth and nineteenth centuries brought a myriad of dignitaries and scholars to Naples, men and women of artistic brilliance and worldly accomplishment. Many of the visitors found Vesuvius and the Roman ruins sobering sights that influenced their lives and their later works.

One of the first was the German poet Johann Wolfgang von Goethe, who arrived from Rome in 1787. The thirty-seven-year-old Goethe was as entranced by Vesuvius as he had been by Emma Hamilton. He climbed the volcano three times, each trip taken in grave peril. Goethe demonstrated extraordinary bravado in ascending Vesuvius while it was erupting, but the role of mountain climber was not natural to the poet's personality.

Earlier, Goethe had confessed to an obsessive fear of heights. As a twenty-year-old law student at the University of Strasburg, he felt crippled by this phobia and set out to conquer it using techniques that we now call behavioral therapy. The treatment consisted of forcing himself to repeatedly climb to a small open platform at the top of a local church where he precariously hung his body over the edge.

Goethe repeated the therapy regularly, then sought a more definitive cure by climbing Europe's highest mountain peaks. He later recounted his cure in his autobiography, *Poetry and Truth:* "There is something about an imminent danger which challenges Man's spirit of contradiction to defy it."

During one particularly violent eruption of Vesuvius, Goethe climbed the volcano with a friend, German artist Johann Tischbein. They hired two local guides who led the way, the clients holding on tightly to their stout leather waistbands. When they reached the upper end of the Atrio del Cavallo, they saw the great cone of Vesuvius above them, throwing out debris in thundering explosions. The four men climbed until they reached a precarious point where volcanic stones fell nearly at their feet.

Goethe then decided to reach the mouth of the crater. The younger of the two guides agreed to accompany him, leaving Tischbein and the other guide behind. They waited until one explosion ended, then set off quickly for the summit, scrambling through a fresh carpet of stone. Climbing arduously until they reached the crater of Vesuvius, they could see steam rise from innumerable fissures. To Goethe, Vesuvius seemed like hell itself. The sight, though hideous, was hypnotic.

Suddenly, a charge of hot stone shot upward past Goethe's face. Lowering their heads, the two men ran downslope, sliding wildly among the loose rocks as volcanic stones rained on them. Fortunately the descent was swift and they reached Tischbein and the other guide safely. Goethe was "happy to have survived."

After this contest with Vesuvius, the German poet had a

clearer vision of why local society seemed so devoted to momentary pleasure. "The Neapolitan would certainly be a different creature if he did not feel himself wedged between God and the Devil," he wrote.

God and the Devil became central literary themes for the emerging genius. Goethe left Naples soon after his encounter with the volcano to continue work on his epic drama *Faust*, in which his antagonist, the devil Mephistopheles, is described in Vesuvian metaphors:

> *The Devils all set up a coughing, sneezing,*
> *At every vent without cessation wheezing;*
> *With sulphur-stench and acids Hell dilated,*
> *And such enormous gas was thence created,*
> *That very soon Earth's level, far extended,*
> *Thick as it was, was heaved, and split, and rended!*

A great many of those who visited Naples were Englishmen, to whom the Grand Tour offered a chance to leave their isolated kingdom. In 1765, young James Boswell, later celebrated as Samuel Johnson's biographer, arrived in Naples to visit John Wilkes, the reformer who had fled England to avoid imprisonment. Like Goethe, Boswell and Wilkes climbed to the top of Vesuvius, finding its sulfurous fumes almost suffocating.

The poet Percy Bysshe Shelley came to Campania in 1818, where he was inspired to write an ode about Pompeii. Shelley had come to live in Italy at the age of twenty-five to escape from Britain, where his liberal atheism was unpopular, and to visit his fellow poet George Gordon Byron, then living in Venice. Captivated by Italy's classical heritage, Shelley toured the country, arriving in the Kingdom of the Two Sicilies in the company of two women, his second wife, Mary, and Byron's mistress, Claire Clairmont.

To visit Vesuvius, Shelley hired mules for himself and Mary in Resina. Claire was placed in a sedan chair and carried up the mountain by four argumentative guides. They passed a wide stream of hardened lava, which impressed Shelley as "an actual image of the waves of the sea, changed into hard black stone by enchantment."

After a brief rest at the hermitage of San Salvatore, near the site of the present Vesuvian Observatory, the party began the final stage of the ascent. They left their mules and the chair at the top of the Atrio del Cavallo and trudged the slope on foot, stepping on boulders to avoid the slippery volcanic ash. At the summit, Shelley stared into the maw of the crater: "After the Glaciers, the most impressive exhibition of the energies of nature I ever saw," he later wrote in a letter to British novelist Thomas Love Peacock.

Shelley journeyed to Pompeii after the New Year of 1819. Though impressed by the ancient town, he was launched into melancholia by the periodic rumblings of Vesuvius. It was in Pompeii that he was inspired to write these lines from his classic *Ode to Naples:*

> *I stood within the city disinterred;*
> *And heard the autumnal leaves like light footfalls*
> *Of spirits passing though the streets; and heard*
> *The Mountain's slumberous voice at intervals*
> *Thrill the roofless halls;*
> *The oracular thunder penetrating shook*
> *The listening soul in my suspended blood;*
> *I felt the Earth out of her deep heart spoke . . .*

A few years later still another Englishman, considerably less poetic than Shelley, came to Naples and explored deeper into the molten innards of Vesuvius than perhaps anyone before or since. Shelley felt the "deep heart" of Vesuvius speak to him; Charles Babbage literally descended into it.

Babbage was an extraordinary man whose accomplishments included the invention of the mechanical calculating machine, the forerunner of the modern electronic computer; the compilation of the first reliable actuarial tables; the invention of the speedometer; and the founding of the Royal Astronomical Society and the Royal Statistical Society. He came to Naples in 1828, only months before beginning his tenure as professor of mathematics at Cambridge University.

The professor brought to Vesuvius a singular analytic curiosity. Accompanied by several local guides, he set out before dawn one morning and reached the summit of the mountain before sunrise. The bottom of the crater, hollowed out by the

1822 eruption, was interlaced with bright red cracks that glowed in the predawn darkness, reminding Babbage of the blood vessels of the human eye. Small explosions periodically shook the stillness.

Babbage toured the circular edge of the crater until sunlight illuminated the scene. He could see that the source of the intermittent explosions was a miniature cone built up around the central vent within the crater. Babbage sought a closer view of the phenomenon, but he was detoured by the five-hundred-foot drop to the crater floor.

He assayed the situation and noticed that layers of lava seemed to have formed a series of ledges along the interior walls of the crater. Babbage thought he might be able to descend into the crater along these ledges with the assistance of ropes. The guides discouraged the plan. None volunteered to accompany the eccentric Englishman, but Babbage finally prevailed upon them to at least lower him into the crater.

He checked his equipment: a heavy barometer, a sextant, thermometers, a tape measure, a few biscuits, a walking stick and vials of smelling salts and ammonia. The guides fashioned a rope harness, slipped it over Babbage, and lowered him to the first ledge. Then, on his own, he leaped from one ledge to the next until he reached the top of a steep, lengthy slope of volcanic ash.

Discarding his rope harness, Babbage stepped into the ash and felt the surface give way beneath his weight. Finding it impossible to stand, he sat down on his backside and careened along the slope toward the volcanic vent until he slid into the small elliptical plain in the center of the crater. He then jumped to his feet and gazed about.

The plain at the bottom of the crater was composed of blackened rock, gutted with irregular ditches from one- to three-feet wide that glowed inside with dull red heat and emitted sulfurous fumes. At the far edge of the plain rose the small active cone that intermittently shot up magma and hot stones.

Babbage began to measure the dimensions of the crater bottom. He thrust his walking stick a few inches into the soil as a reference point for his trigonometric calculations, but in moments it kindled into flame. The mathematician then turned his attention to another analytic proposition. How could he manage to peer down into a live magma chamber at molten lava that had not yet reached the surface of the crater? Was there enough time between eruptions to permit an approach to the very edge of the live vent?

Babbage stood quietly as volcanic mists rose around him. He calculated that the small cone erupted at intervals of ten to fifteen minutes, lapsing into repose between explosions. Gaining confidence in his data, Babbage dared an approach. He waited until an explosive cycle had spent itself, then rushed forward through a crevice in the side of the cone, hoping to peer down into the magma chamber. But a large projecting boulder lodged in the vent forty feet below blocked his view of the molten reservoir. Babbage quickly retreated and waited at a safe distance for the next explosion.

With heightened determination, he timed several more cycles to check his previous calculations, confirming that there was a minimum of ten minutes between explosions. He would allow himself six minutes to observe the magma and four to escape to safety. As one explosive cycle ended, he noted the time on his watch, then raced for the cone.

To the consternation of the guides watching from five hundred feet above, Babbage edged through the gash and stepped carefully down the rocks that lined the inside of the vent until he reached the boulder that had blocked his view. He was now forty feet below the crater bottom, deep within the core of Vesuvius, only a few feet above the molten reservoir.

Dropping flat upon the boulder, Babbage peered over the edge into a glowing lake of orange lava, searing heat and fumes rising into his face. As Babbage watched, a small bubble formed on the surface of the magma and grew menacingly larger, threatening to burst the molten rock upward. Babbage nervously checked his watch. Barely a minute had passed since the end of the last explosive cycle. Relying on his calculations and ignoring the visible signs of danger, he resolved to remain where he was. His analysis had been correct: Slowly the orange bubble subsided quietly back into the magma.

So transfixed was Babbage that he only now realized that the boulder was scorching his clothes. Looking about, he located a ledge a few feet higher where he could stand and still see the activity below. More bubbles appeared in the lake, each one growing larger than before, but they too sank harmlessly back into the magma.

The minutes ticked off on Babbage's watch as the scorching liquid rock bubbled up with increasing force. Babbage felt suffocated from the hellish vapors that burned into his nostrils, but he revived himself with his supply of smelling salts. He found himself nearly hypnotized into immobility by the sight no one else had ever seen, the inner pulsations of Vesuvius. Each bright orange bubble of magma threatened to be the one that would explode upward, incinerating the presumptuous human.

Six minutes, Babbage's limit, had passed. Lightheaded from the vapors and exhausted by the heat, Babbage forced himself to move, climbing back up the rocky outcroppings on the inner face of the vent until he reached the crater floor forty feet above. He squeezed back through the opening in the side of the cone and ran for the far side of the crater. He reached safety shortly before lava and smoke shot up through the channel in which he had crouched. As Babbage had calculated, a total of ten minutes had passed.

Later, when he returned to his hotel in Naples and pulled off his thick boots, the leather fell to pieces in his hand.

Several had written odes about Vesuvius, but no visitor had considered the dramatic possibilities inherent in the ancient ruins at Pompeii and Herculaneum. Sir Walter Scott, ailing and penniless despite the success of *Ivanhoe*, visited Pompeii in 1833. He was overcome with melancholy. Crying "This is the city of the dead," he had to be carried away.

But another British author who arrived that same year saw Pompeii as the ideal fictional setting for a romantic historical novel. Edward Bulwer was a dashing, thirty-year-old Member of Parliament who had gained a following at home for such gossipy society novels as *Pelham*, *Eugene Aram* and *Godolphin*.

Bulwer had found the Grand Tour burdensome by the time he reached the southern Italian kingdom. Fatigued the day his party visited the ruins of ancient Pompeii, he told his friends to go through the city without him while he rested upon a bench. An archaeologist, Antonio Bonucci, who happened to pass where Bulwer sat, initiated a conversation about the city. Bonucci's descriptions of ancient Pompeii seemed to bring the gray ruins to life, and Bulwer readily accepted the offer of a private tour with his educated guide.

The two men walked to the Villa of Diomed, where Bonucci led the writer to its subterranean vault in which eighteen skeletons had been unearthed. "The sand," Bulwer later wrote, "consolidated by damps, had taken the forms of the skeletons as in a cast, and the traveller may yet see the impression of a female neck and bosom of young and rounded proportions. . . ."

The young Englishman now grasped the literary potential of the great eruption. As they were crossing the Forum, Bonucci showed him where excavators had found the skeleton of a man crushed in two by a falling marble column. The man's skull was exceptionally large. In the dungeonlike cellar of the Temple of Isis, Bulwer saw ax marks on the wall where a trapped priest had attempted to chop his way out.

Returning to England with voluminous notes, Bulwer quickly fashioned a story. The man with the huge skull became Arbaces, wicked high priest of Isis. The trapped priest with the axe was Burbo, whom Arbaces had confined to the temple to further his plot to marry the fair Ione. The impression of the full girlish bosom materialized into the beautiful, scandalous Julia. Bulwer created a hero, Glaucus, and gave him a real home in Pompeii, known as the House of the Tragic Poet. Bulwer's classic novel *The Last Days of Pompeii* appeared in print the year after his visit, 1834, and became an instant success.

The novelist had created a credible account, for his time, of the cataclysm of A.D. 79, but updated analysis shows several fundamental errors. For dramatic effect Bulwer brought the Pompeiians to the Amphitheatre for a gladiatorial contest during which the hero, Glaucus, was to be thrown to the lions. In *The Last Days*, Vesuvius ostensibly erupts while the Amphitheatre is crowded with spectators. The novelist probably drew upon the erroneous report by the Roman historian Dio Cassius Cocceianus, which stated that Pompeii had been destroyed while its entire population was gathered in the Amphitheatre.

The excavations proved this untrue. No bodies were found there, a fact that Bulwer was aware of at the time he composed his epic. Bulwer has his hero view the collapse of the old peak of Mount Somma and the rise of the new central cone. During the course of the eruption, it was unlikely that any Pompeiians could witness the event amid the volcanic darkness.

Despite Bulwer's errors, the success of *The Last Days of Pompeii* heightened public awareness of volcanic power and made Pompeii and Vesuvius required stops on the Grand Tour.

A decade later, another British novelist, the prolific Charles Dickens, visited Italy. In 1844, at the age of thirty-two, Dickens moved with his family to Italy for a year, "to stroll about, wherever his restless humor carried him," as he put it.

Soon after his arrival in Naples, he toured Pompeii. But like many others, Dickens was drawn to Vesuvius. "The mountain is the genius of the scene," he wrote. Though it was winter and Vesuvius was capped with snow, Dickens insisted on climbing the volcano that very day. There were several others in his party, including two women and a local gentleman referred to acidly by Dickens as "Mr. Pickle of Portici." Dickens persuaded them that, despite the cold, it would be fascinating to view the sunset from halfway up Vesuvius, to see the moon overhead at the summit, then to descend at midnight.

The party began its climb up narrow stony lanes, emerging into a bleak region of lava, which Dickens wrote, looked "as if the earth had been ploughed up by burning thunderbolts." The procession halted to gaze at the sun as it set in the Bay of Naples, transforming the slopes of Vesuvius into a wasteland.

In darkness, Dickens and his party moved slowly up a lava-strewn pathway, eventually reaching the steep slope at the base of the central cone. Dim light was reflected by the snow that covered the upper portions of Vesuvius. Frigid air pierced the clothing of the climbers.

Dickens dismounted his pony while guides prepared litters: two for the women and a third for one gentleman so heavy that fifteen men were required to carry him to the summit. Dickens and the others walked with staves. The rising moon bathed Vesuvius in gentle light and revived the spirits of the adventurers, who finally reached the edge of the crater, now almost filled with lava.

Dickens felt Vesuvius drawing at him. "There is something in the fire and roar that generate an irresistible desire to get nearer to it," he wrote. But only one companion and the head guide shared Dickens' compulsion to see the Vesuvian fire at close range. On hands and knees the three men crawled toward the small active cone, the other guides calling loudly for them to return.

Their cries only stimulated Dickens' resolve. The knees of their britches torn, the three men continued their crawl across the hot plain until they reached the base of the small volcanic cone. They climbed up to its lips, then stared into "the Hell of boiling fire below." The orange glow lit their faces as if they were poised above a blast furnace. They could remain for only a moment. Giddy with accomplishment, their clothes blackened, they tumbled back down and rejoined their party.

It was time to descend the mountain. Now their foe was not heat but ice. Climbers could usually slide downslope through the loose ash but the ice made such a strategy impossible. Instead, a dozen guides formed a human chain with the man at the front beating a rough trail with his stick. The rest followed carefully down the slick path, frequently slipping to their knees.

The peculiar procession organized by Dickens moved slowly down Vesuvius through the freezing night. Those in front were often pushed onto the ice by others who fell behind them, grabbing their ankles for support. Dickens' spirits ran high. He had risked his life to peer into the vent of Vesuvius and had survived. Frequent falls in the snow could now only strengthen his good humor.

Now, walking alongside Dickens, Mr. Pickle of Portici suddenly stumbled and fell to the ice, plunging headfirst down the mountain. Bouncing like a human snowball for hundreds of feet, he came to rest near the edge of the Atrio del Cavallo. Almost simultaneously, one of the guides rolled past Dickens, followed by the hurtling form of a small boy, one of the guides' children. These two also rolled down the ice until they joined Mr. Pickle at the point where the party had left the ponies.

The procession worked its way anxiously down to the Atrio del Cavallo, where Mr. Pickle and the others were waiting, their clothes torn and stained with blood. Fortunately, the snow had cushioned much of the impact, and no one had suffered serious injury. Once below the ice line, the Dickens party made its way easily to the Hermitage of San Salvatore, where they were provided with food and a blazing fire.

Stimulated by Vesuvius, tourism flourished in Naples. England's Queen Victoria visited the southern Italian kingdom in 1838. Mexico's future emperor, Ferdinand Maximilian, toured Pompeii in 1851. About the same time, American author Herman Melville arrived for a short vacation before returning home to begin work on *Moby Dick*.

In 1867, another American writer, Mark Twain, came to Naples. He was then a thirty-one-year-old reporter for the *San Francisco Alta California* and suspicious of sophisticated travel articles that glorified the wonders of the Grand Tour. He was determined, he said, "to suggest to the reader how *he* would be likely to see Europe and the East if he looked at them with his own eyes. . . ."

Twain found Pompeii and Vesuvius deeply moving sights, stops on the Grand Tour that did live up to their reputations. But their glory could not curb his biting wit. Walking through Pompeii, he tripped in one of the deep wheel ruts in the ancient stone streets and cursed the "inborn nature of Street Commissioners to shirk their duty." Later, when he viewed a body cast, his anger was dispelled by the happy thought that this was the remains of Pompeii's Street Commissioner. He also directed acid comments at the tour guides, who expected constant tips.

Vesuvius and its ancient victim brought a new perspective to the maturing writer. After viewing the ruins of Pompeii, Twain reevaluated the importance of seeking immortality. He wrote:

> . . . one thing strikes me with a force it never had before: the unsubstantial, unlasting character of fame. Men lived

long lives, in the olden time, and struggled feverishly through them, toiling like slaves, in oratory, in generalship, or in literature, and then laid down and died, happy in the possession of an enduring history and a deathless name. Well, twenty little centuries flutter away, and what is left of these things? A crazy inscription on a block of stone, which stuffy antiquaries bother over and tangle up and make nothing out of but a bare name (which they spell wrong)—no history, no tradition, no poetry—nothing can give it even passing interest. . . . These thoughts sadden me. I will to bed.

Twain ascended Vesuvius on mule-back in the company of guides. On top, he viewed the crater in the early morning sun. The circular pit seemed to form a circus ring, muted by velvet moss frosted with shining dust. In the center of this setting was the one-hundred-foot inner cone, crusted over with minerals that glowed variegated shades of red, blue, brown, black, yellow and white. Wrote Twain: ". . . when the sun burst through the morning mists and fired this tinted magnificence, it topped imperial Vesuvius like a jeweled crown!"

Mark Twain had approached Vesuvius, as he had the other stops on the Grand Tour, with Yankee skepticism. But the majesty of the great volcano had captured his soul. He gazed at the contrast of colors and remarked, "One could stand and look down upon it for a week without getting tired of it."

16

SCIENCE COMES
TO VESUVIUS

An orderly double row of volcanic bombs, some half as large as a man, today guards the stone stairway leading to the old red-brick Royal Vesuvian Observatory. The building stands slightly uphill from the modern concrete observatory, not far from the summit of the volcano.

A massive ironclad door swings open into the partially abandoned shell of the world's first permanent volcanic monitoring station. Since the old building is closer to the crater than the new one, it is used to house the communications equipment that collects data from a ring of seismographs along the upper slopes. The equipment occupies only a rooftop area and a single side room, leaving the remainder of the structure a dusty museum crammed with outdated volcanic measuring devices, faded yellow seismic charts, photographs and other mementos of past eruptions.

In the foyer stand bronze busts of previous directors. It was in this observatory that volcanologists continued the work of scientific observation in the tradition of Sir William Hamilton, and they took the first steps toward the goal of predicting an eruption. Today that objective is a partial reality, demonstrated by the clear warnings issued by scientists monitoring Mount St. Helens.

But volcanology and archaeology have not always been advanced disciplines. Transforming the often haphazard excavations at Pompeii and Herculaneum into true scientific endeavors took a century of effort, work that was aided by almost continual activity within Vesuvius.

Vesuvius had been agitated during the first part of the nineteenth century, building up for the first eruption to occur during the reign of Ferdinand II, monarch of the newly named Kingdom of the Two Sicilies. That explosive event would help to revolutionize the scientific study of volcanoes and make the politically reactionary king a cultural benefactor.

In August 1834, a gash appeared on the eastern slope of Vesuvius, from which lava flowed heavily into the Valley of the Inferno, then diverged into two streams. One stream threatened to rebury the ruins of Pompeii, but the lava stopped short near the village of Boscoreale. The other, larger, flow moved across the village of Caposecchi, crushing all but four of the five hundred homes.

As Ferdinand saw his people grieving, he wondered how long they must endure the power of Vesuvius. Must mankind be forever subject to nature's caprice? Was this not the Age of Science?

More than a half century earlier a Scotsman, James Hutton, set forth his concept of uniformitarianism, which became the foundation theory of modern geology. Hutton saw volcanoes and earthquakes not as isolated accidents, but as manifestations of ongoing earth processes. He believed that careful study of these phenomena could result in reducing their awesome consequences.

Britain's Sir Charles Lyell elaborated on this theory in his classic *Principles of Geology*, published in 1830. Lyell combed Vesuvius in 1828, then compared the towns now adjacent to Vesuvius with Pompeii and Herculaneum. He speculated that future observers would see new ruins where towns now stood. "The geologist will then behold the towns . . . laid open in the steep cliffs, where he will discover streets superimposed above each other, with thick intervening strata of tuff or lava," Lyell predicted. "Among the ruins will he see skeletons of men, and impressions of the human form stamped in solid rocks."

Ferdinand II was aware of these advances in geologic thought, and believed that increased understanding of Vesuvius was the only hope of controlling his resident demon. In 1844, he established the Royal Vesuvian Observatory at a strategically shielded point a little more than one thousand feet below the summit. To the position of first director, he named

Macedonio Melloni, who immediately began to collect systematic data on the daily activity of Vesuvius.

The excavations at Pompeii and Herculaneum were in the same need of scientific discipline. In 1860 they came under the direction of two noted men, one a prominent literary figure, the other someone who was to finally bring a sense of science to the ancient sites. The catalyst was the unconventional political leader, Giuseppe Garibaldi, head of northern Italy's Free Party, who amassed a volunteer army of a thousand men in an attempt to liberate the Two Sicilies from the Bourbons and to unite the Italian peninsula.

The prominent author Alexandre Dumas was drawn into that struggle, then into the story of Vesuvius. Dumas longed to recreate his days of literary glory during the reign of France's Louis Philippe, the Citizen King. It was in the 1840s that Dumas had written his narrative hymns to the triumph of swashbuckling good over dictatorial evil: *The Three Musketeers* and *The Count of Monte Cristo*. But by 1860, at fifty, his life had soured.

His fortune was squandered and his work ignored. His bastard son and namesake, Alexandre Dumas, *fils*, was now receiving the riches and, worse, praise for the play *Camille*. The elder Dumas decided he needed a change and embarked from Marseille upon his yacht *Emma*, named to honor his current love, the actress Emilie Cordier.

Dumas' destination was Egypt, but when the yacht docked temporarily at Genoa, he changed plans. All Genoa was excited by the recent departure of Garibaldi for Sicily. To Dumas it represented revolution and irresistible adventure, and he set sail for Palermo, Sicily, where Garibaldi accepted the aid of the willing Frenchman.

Garibaldi quickly took Sicily and moved north along the mainland toward Naples. Dumas followed, acting as liaison with foreign governments, here accepting the surrender of a loyalist regiment, there editing the terms of a peace treaty. When Naples capitulated to Garibaldi in September 1860 and the Bourbons were deposed, Garibaldi rewarded the Frenchman by appointing him director of excavations at Pompeii and Herculaneum.

Ensconced in a Neapolitan palace, Dumas made plans to invite French scholars to systematize the archaeological work. But he had little opportunity to implement his plan. Garibaldi retired, proposing Victor Emmanuel II, King of Sardinia, as ruler of a united Italy. With his political mentor gone, Dumas soon realized that he had underestimated the new Italian nationalism. One night he heard a crowd demonstrating outside his elegant palace apartments.

"Away with Dumas!" came the shouts. The riot was put down, but Dumas saw the futility of his position. He avoided the excavations, concentrating on cataloging the ribald art locked in the basement of the National Museum, until King Victor Emmanuel replaced him with thirty-seven-year-old Giuseppe Fiorelli. Dumas lived and wrote in Naples for the next several years, but could never recapture his former eminence.

It was Dumas' successor, Fiorelli, who finally brought a systematic scientific approach to the excavations. His first accomplishment was the removal of debris that had been heaped onto excavated areas. He then divided Pompeii into regions and blocks, numbering each building, a classification system still in use today. Another important contribution was the *Journal of the Excavation of Pompeii*, which recorded each discovery and its exact location.

Fiorelli's historic innovation was made in 1864, when a work crew, digging in the cellar of a home near the Stabian Baths at Pompeii, unearthed a portion of a skeleton. They immediately called Fiorelli, who carefully enlarged the hole where the body lay. Inside he could see a skull and a mass of bones within a cavity whose surfaces bore the exact outlines of a human shape, complete to a detailed imprint of its outer garments, hair, jewelry, even facial expressions. The cavity had been formed by the decomposition of the body within the hard volcanic ground, leaving a ghostly human impression surrounding the isolated bones.

Fiorelli decided to re-create the victim of Vesuvius in a full-size cast by filling the hole with plaster of Paris. After it had dried, his workers carefully chipped away the surrounding dirt to reveal the three-dimensional image of a Pompeiian woman, now preserved exactly as she had been at the moment of death.

Within days, four human figures were recreated in the cellar. One woman had two silver rings circling the bones of her fingers. One arm was broken, the other raised in useless resistance to her fate. A girl, about fourteen years old, lay behind the woman, resting her head upon her own arms. Perhaps the two were mother and daughter. Nearby was the body of another woman, poorly attired. The fourth cast revealed the form of a huge, broad man, an iron ring on his finger, his feet clad in sandals.

As Fiorelli gazed at these first body casts, he knew he had devised an archaeological technique both grisly and fascinating, one that would add immeasurably to the lore of Pompeii and demonstrate, through a graphic record of horror, the true power of Vesuvius.

The Vesuvian Observatory was now under the direction of Luigi Palmieri, an experienced seismologist who installed the latest equipment to monitor Vesuvius. Palmieri spent long hours reflecting upon the periodic nature of the volcano and became convinced that Vesuvian eruptions followed a pattern that could be charted and forecast.

Palmieri's theory was reinforced by events. During a two-year period, 1865 to 1867, earthquakes hit the middle Mediterranean basin. Palmieri soon heard of the volcanic eruptions of Etna, Santorini, Hekla and the Azores. All of these, he was convinced, were related to his observations at the summit of Vesuvius, barely one thousand feet above his office.

In the autumn of 1867, Palmieri's seismographs began to register increasing subterranean shocks. The new equipment proved to be accurate: The volcano erupted during the night of November 14–15, circling the mountain with an igneous glow. For a full month the volcano was a dazzling spectacle, effusing thirteen separate lava streams down its slopes. Their jagged flows became interlaced with the mountain's winter snow, forming orange cascades where the molten rock poured over small cliffs.

Palmieri kept meticulous records of the explosions, which demonstrated a clear daily pattern. During each twenty-four hours, there were two periods when the lava flows were more copious and the steam and ash clouds more forceful. As he charted the cycle he realized that these maximum periods occurred at a later time each day. Checking tide tables, Palmieri realized that Vesuvius was affected by the pull of the moon, the eruptions increasing whenever the lunar face was new or full.

Knowledge of Vesuvius was evolving, but with agonizing slowness. Palmieri's discovery was helpful during an eruption, but he knew there was more long-range data Vesuvius could reveal. As the mountain grew quiet, Palmieri returned to his data, searching for the key to the ultimate question: How could one predict when Vesuvius would next erupt?

Palmieri reviewed the history of Vesuvius since its awakening in 1631. The volcano acted in broad cycles, each consisting of three stages that inevitably culminated in a great eruption, what he termed "a paroxysmal explosion." The first stage is a period of dormancy that follows every great eruption: It typically lasts from eighteen months to a maximum of seven and a half years.

In the second stage, that of cone building, Vesuvius slowly becomes renewed. Lava oozes into the open crater left by the previous explosion, gradually filling the pit and clogging the central vent. This stage transforms the crater into a raised plateau, from which internal cones build up as a result of mild internal pressure.

The third, or explosive, stage appears after years of moderate activity during which the clogged vent of Vesuvius is ripped open by the accumulated rising of subterranean magma. Seismic activity increases markedly as the mantle of white steam changes to black. In the final act, Vesuvius explodes with lethal energy, expelling lava rapidly from the cone and from side fissures and venting enormous quantities of gas, which create the characteristic mushroom cloud of ash. Volcanic bombs, pyroclastic flows, torrential thunderstorms and mudflows are all associated with this harrowing final stage. At the end, the volcanic crater is once more an empty shell, and Vesuvius sinks into repose to begin still another cycle.

Palmieri believed that Vesuvian cycles were decipherable and that they reappeared with regularity. He noted that paroxysmal explosions had occurred in 1660, 1682, 1698, 1707, 1737, 1760, 1766, 1779, 1794, 1822, 1834, 1839, 1850, 1855,

1861 and 1868. The period of the cycles had lasted from four to thirty years, the average being about twelve years between explosions.

Palmieri's calculations of the Vesuvian cycle were tentative, for as the volcano continued to erupt, they had to be adjusted and clarified. But Luigi Palmieri, the second director of the Vesuvian Observatory, had begun the first scientific inquiry into the true behavior of the great volcano.

Vesuvius remained dormant for several years after the 1868 eruption, but Palmieri's seismographs then began to record increasing activity in the magma chamber. Early in the morning on April 26, 1872, Vesuvius came to life with an explosion, followed by an emission of swift running lava that overflowed the crater on several sides. Studying the lava's unusual speed, Palmieri calculated that if it continued at its present velocity, it would burst into Naples within twenty-four hours. In that city, the terrified populace remained indoors.

On the small bridge of Casanova, which separates Naples from its southernmost suburb of San Giorgio a Cremano, a larger-than-life statue of San Gennaro gazes sternly at the mountain. Some Neapolitans still believe that the statue originally stood with its arms at its sides, but it is said that on this night in 1872, the statue raised its right arm toward Vesuvius, freezing it into the position it holds today. In any event, the lava halted hours later in the Naples suburb, and the city was spared.

As Vesuvius once more sank into tranquillity, the people surrounding it sought to capitalize upon its fame. It was soon easier than ever to visit Vesuvius: From Naples the tourist could now ride the Circumvesuviana Railway to Resina and catch the Vesuvian Railway to the terminal station only a short distance from the observatory. No longer did visitors have to climb the final slope on foot. With much fanfare, a funicular railway was opened to carry passengers the final thousand feet up to the summit. A song was commissioned for the grand opening and "Funiculi Funicula" became an international hit.

Not long after Luigi Palmieri died in 1896, Professor R. V. Matteucci, a stocky man with silver handlebar mustaches, was named director of the observatory. Like his spiritual predecessor, Sir William Hamilton, Matteucci became slavishly devoted to Vesuvius, often camping out near the summit to view volcanic displays up close. One night in 1900, he slipped and fell into a fresh mound of scorching ash, burning himself badly.

But the accident did not weaken his ardor. In *The Cosmopolitan* magazine, the professor characterized Vesuvius as his mercurial mistress:

> I love my mountain. She and I dwell together in solitude mysterious and terrible. . . . I could not leave her. I am wedded to her forever; my few friends say that her breath will scorch and wither my poor life one of these days; that she will bury my house in streams of liquid metal or raze it to its very foundation. Already she has hurt me, has injured me sorely. Yet I forgive her, I wait upon her, I am hers always.

After the eruption of 1872, Vesuvius was quiescent for several years, until it began the three-stage process outlined by Palmieri that would culminate in the next great eruption, that of 1906. This eruption was to be witnessed by a scientist destined to become a new Vesuvian devotee, an American expatriate named Frank Perret. A technician trained by Thomas Alva Edison, Perret found the fervid pace of Edison's work detrimental to his health, and in 1903, at the age of forty-one, he retired to a seaside retreat near Naples.

He was soon captivated by the volcano's brilliant nighttime displays of incandescent gas, and was such a frequent visitor to the observatory that Matteucci offered him the post of honorary assistant. Perret accepted and worked alongside the director for several years, absorbing volcanology on the job.

The long-awaited explosion predicted by Palmieri's theory occurred on the morning of April 4, 1906. Two days later, Perret and Matteucci climbed to the source of the flow halfway up the volcano, where highly incandescent molten rock poured from the mouth of a cave at the speed of six hundred feet per hour. As the volcanologists measured the flow, they heard solid rock tear open above them. A sheet of lava shot

fifteen feet upward, then flowed down in the direction of Boscotrecase. The following night, a towering fire obliterated the
village and melted the tracks of the Circumvesuviana Railway.

Shortly after midnight the next day, April 8, Palm Sunday,
1906, severe explosions made it impossible to stand firm
within the observatory. Large cracks appeared in the observatory walls, and Matteucci's sensitive seismic instruments
were thrown into disarray. Fearing the building's collapse,
Matteucci, Perret, and a handful of carabinieri ran outside to
seek shelter in a small open chalet nearby. The observatory
crew huddled together as each earthquake explosion caused
deafening thunderclaps.

At 2:30 A.M. a powerful tremor knocked Perret and the others to the ground of their wooden chalet. Looking to Vesuvius,
Perret saw an upper portion of the great cone crumble, causing
the pressure upon the vent to increase further. During the
night nearly four feet of volcanic fallout buried the village of
Ottaviano, crushing the roofs of ten homes and five churches
and killing at least fifty people. In nearby San Giuseppe, two
hundred of the residents were gathered in the local cathedral
when the aging structure toppled in upon them.

At 3:30 A.M. the accumulated pressure within the volcanic
cone caused the entire upper rim to give way. By later that
morning, the earth shocks had decreased in intensity, but Vesuvius was still fired by an enormous reservoir of pressurized
gas that soared several miles into the air. At the top of this
huge column globules of gas exploded in cauliflowerlike puffs.

Perret was overcome by the magnificence of the display. He
wrote that "the events . . . seemed to show that—even as the
younger Pliny wrote of similar conditions in this same region
nearly two thousand years ago—'the last eternal night of story
has settled on the world.' "

Perret decided to go down the mountain and return to Naples, a city he found in a state of panic: A tenth of the populace
had fled. The eruption had already claimed its first victims in
the city. The Mount Oliveto Market, a large enclosed structure, collapsed from the cumulative effect of the earth
tremors, killing fourteen. Perret spent the night in Naples, but
when he awoke, he hired a horse-drawn cab to take him back

to the observatory. Near Resina the cab encountered such a thick fall of ash that the horse could go no farther. Perret decided to climb the mountain, and as he walked through darkness he was aware of terrorized faces peering at him from doorways. Who was this strange man climbing Vesuvius in the midst of a conflagration?

At the observatory Matteucci greeted Perret warmly, never expecting his return. Ten people—including the railroad stationmaster, a telegrapher, a brigadier and five of his carabinieri —were now closeted in the damaged observatory building, supplied with scanty rations. They sat in darkness for the next thirty-six hours, watching the ash build up outside to a height of two feet. On April 10, army sappers cleared the heavy buildup off the observatory roof. From one terrace alone the troops removed six tons of debris.

Still the great volcano continued its massive bombardment. On the morning of April 13, Perret watched as a boiling pyroclastic flow shook loose from the upper slopes and descended along a path directly toward the observatory. The flow crashed into the Calle Umberto and nearly surmounted it but was deflected to the west, passing safely below the observatory. The flaming rock had covered nearly a mile in the space of a few seconds.

At noon, on April 18, as a great cloud once again moved over the observatory, Perret and the others suddenly noticed an unusual warmth about their feet and legs. Breathing became difficult, and "an indescribable feeling of oppression" overcame them. The volcanologists recognized these as the symptoms of carbon dioxide poisoning. There was no escape; they could only hope that the carbon dioxide content would not reach the suffocation level.

The carabinieri now decided to bring in neighboring families whose homes were in jeopardy. Tying everyone to a long rope, they moved, snakelike, to the observatory, the only haven on the torn mountainside. Forty people were soon crowded into the building, including one woman and several children. Days passed as the eruption gradually subsided.

On April 22, they received a surprise visit from the Duke and Duchess of Aosta who brought news that the vigilance of the observatory crew had promoted calm in Naples; their daily telegraphic reports had cheered the frightened populace. Five hundred people had died in the surrounding villages, they told the observatory survivors. But if these brave observers on the slopes of Vesuvius itself could endure the eruption, surely the Neapolitans could also survive.

Over the next few years, the local villagers rebuilt. King Victor Emmanuel decorated Matteucci with the rank of Commander of the Order of the Crown. Matteucci retired soon after and was succeeded as observatory director by Professor Giuseppe Imbo. Frank Perret founded a volcanological museum at St. Pierre, Martinique, site of the devastating 1902 eruption of Mount Pelée, and became a renowned U.S. volcanologist.

And Vesuvius once more lapsed into repose. Thirty-four years had passed between the eruption of 1872 and 1906. Another cycle had ended; another was to begin.

17

VESUVIUS LIVES

VESUVIUS WAS ONLY moderately active in the years following 1906, then the volcano reawoke in the midst of World War II and demonstrated its power to a skeptical modern world.

During the thirty-eight-year hiatus, only one man, Dr. Giuseppe Imbo, director of the observatory, had scrupulously monitored the volcano's inner pressure. From his isolated post he checked his seismic charts daily, measuring the growth of a lava lake in the central crater, walking over the crunchy, disintegrating lava beds of numberless past eruptions to chart the morphology of the mountain. It was all done in the hope of predicting the next eruption and to gain early warning of the path of future lava flows. Meanwhile, he waited patiently for the inevitable.

At dawn on September 9, 1943, the United States VI Corps and the British X Corps assaulted the beaches of Salerno, immediately south of the Bay of Naples. Three months earlier, Mussolini's dictatorship had toppled. Although the new government surrendered to the Allies and joined them as co-belligerents the night before the invasion, Italy remained under the control of the occupying German troops.

The enemy realized the importance of the upcoming battle for Naples, garrisoning the city with its Hermann Goering Panzer Division. Field Marshal Albert Kesselring ordered his tanks to counterattack the Allied troops at Ponte Bruciato, south of Salerno. The Germans pushed the Allies into a retreat toward the sea until the U.S. commander, Lieutenant General Mark W. Clark, halted the German counterattack five miles short of the coast. One week after landing at Salerno, Clark had driven the Germans north.

The battle moved across the slopes of Vesuvius for the next two weeks. It was not the first time that the volcano had played a role in Allied war plans. In 1940, the British had proposed that the crater of Vesuvius be bombed, hoping to cause a catastrophic eruption that would disrupt strategic shipping activities at Naples. The plan was reportedly discarded as impractical, but Professor Imbo could not be sure it had never been attempted. He had recorded significant seismic activity in November 1941, and suspected that it had been caused by an Allied bomb dropped into the crater. Vesuvius, its inner cone glowing at night from subterranean fires, seemed an irresistible target.

In September of 1943, Vesuvius stood in the path to Naples. The Allies moved from village to village fighting a German rear guard that used the mountain's contours for its defense. The Allies finally entered Naples on October 3, 1943, and by early 1944 the long war had ended for the Campanians.

Vesuvius had accommodated the Allies with its inactivity. But on the night of January 8, 1944, there was a disquieting portent as Vesuvius came to life. Two separate streams of orange-hued molten rock moved downward following the contours of the land, until they converged four hundred feet below the crest. In Naples the two glowing flows of lava appeared to form a huge burning "V." The Italians were accustomed to minor volcanic displays, and they shrugged, calling it an omen of an early Allied victory.

Professor Imbo was monitoring this activity, but his studies were disturbed one winter morning by the roar of military Jeeps. U.S. Army Air Force enlisted men moved officiously through the front door of the red-brick observatory waving requisition papers. Relegating the professor and his seismographs to a corner, the Americans carried in a cache of electronic equipment. Sensitive radio receivers were ensconced in the fourth-floor belfrylike tower. The unit's secret mission was to contact Allied agents behind enemy lines to prepare long-range weather forecasts for D-day.

At first irritated by the intrusion, Imbo became friendly

with the Americans over the next weeks. In turn they did their best not to interfere with his work, and once again he returned to the mountain. In February and March it quivered beneath his feet as his instruments measured significant seismic activity. Convinced that a major eruption was imminent, Imbo walked up and down Vesuvius several times to warn the villagers in the valleys below.

On March 12, 1944, with an intimidating roar, boulders were rent from the inner facing of the central cone and fell in upon the volcano. Tons of rock now dammed the escape vents of the subterranean gases that fired the volcano. Blocked from free access, the gases slowly pressurized at the base of the chamber several miles below the Bay of Naples, accumulating sufficient energy to blast through. The question was not if, but when, the volcano would erupt. How devastating would be this latest manifestation of the ancient power of Vesuvius?

The professor moved into a small room at the observatory, where, sleeping next to his seismographs, he waited. Imbo's problems were overwhelming. He had no car, and to reach the trembling four-thousand-foot-high summit of Vesuvius for his daily observations he had to walk miles of road circling upward from the observatory. His invaluable seismic charts could not be preserved without alcohol, which was then unavailable.

He confided his anxieties to Staff Sergeant Fred Drake, the senior enlisted man. "An eruption is imminent," the professor warned him. He pointed to the smoke rising from Vesuvius' cone which each day seemed to darken. It had been white a week earlier; now it was charcoal gray. "That's an indication that something is happening," he told the sergeant. Drake had already seen the power of Vesuvius in the death casts at Pompeii, solemn evidence of the volcano's potential. As the smoke grew denser each day, some of Drake's men wanted to leave, but the squadron's work could not be stopped, even for a volcano.

The volume of lava increased to a point that signaled the beginning of a major eruption, but Imbo's observatory measurements were insufficient. He realized that there was no better method of gathering data than to personally confront the molten streams that now moved down the mountainside.

As night closed in, Imbo raced on foot to the Hotel Eremo and dashed into the dining room, breathless. "Please!" he implored. "I need somebody to drive me as far as the road will go."

"I'll go with you," Drake volunteered.

The airman commandeered a Jeep and drove up the road, stopping a few yards short of the path of the oncoming lava. The two men began to climb up along a ridge of old lava, with Imbo in the lead, carrying a heavy load of portable scientific instruments. Gravel loosened under them, forcing the two men to their knees repeatedly, but they moved ahead, keeping to high ground to avoid any sudden lava flow. The professor struggled to within a hundred feet of the edge of the rim.

"This is far enough," he said, motioning Drake to halt. For a time the heat seemed to weld the two men in place as they viewed a sight few had ever witnessed at such close range. The panorama of an erupting volcano lay before them. Imbo and Drake suddenly shared an irrational fear: Would Vesuvius retaliate for their impertinence?

As if in answer, the mountain issued a thunderclap. The men watched as a glowing boulder, twelve feet in diameter, arched a hundred feet into the air. The huge missile floated off to the right, struck the ground, then bounced erratically down the slope, showering orange sparks.

"What am I doing here?" Drake suddenly exclaimed. "Come on, professor, let's get off the mountain!"

Imbo was not ready to leave. For decades, he had prepared for this event, the next great eruption of Vesuvius. It was as though the mountain had called him out for individual combat. Ignoring the boulders that flew overhead, Imbo set off directly toward the lava flow. Drake was unsure of making his way back alone, and had no other choice than to follow the volcanologist.

The professor edged his way toward the lava, which was moving downslope at the speed of a fast walk. The smell of sulfur was nauseating. Oblivious to the danger, Imbo pierced the skin of the lava with a pincerlike instrument, then peered at the glow through a spectroscope. "I'm taking the temperature and trying to gauge the speed and composition of the lava," he explained to Drake. Here near the summit, the professor added, the flow was only about a foot deep, but if Vesuvius continued to erupt, the lava could build into a moving wall twenty feet high that would incinerate anything it encountered.

As if to emphasize Imbo's point, Vesuvius suddenly issued another boulder, which arched over the heads of the two men, then crashed squarely onto the tracks of the funicular railway that had carried generations of tourists to the summit. Within moments after the bomb fell, the lava flow also assaulted the funicular, engulfing the already mangled tracks.

Ignoring the heat and fumes, Imbo moved up and down the slope near the lava, recording the data he needed to forecast the lava's probable course, and with it the threat to the darkened villages below. Drake remained at the professor's side for hours, anxious to quit this hell but unable to persuade Imbo to leave. Drake's throat was singed from the heat and the acrid sulfur fumes. Each time Vesuvius roared, both men peered over their shoulders, checking the trajectories of the volcanic bombs that spewed into the night.

It was well after midnight when Imbo finally turned to leave, now convinced that within twenty-four hours the eruption would seriously threaten the countryside. The two men slid through old lava flows down to their Jeep and drove back to the Hotel Eremo. Exhausted, Drake fell into bed as Professor Imbo returned to the observatory and his vigil.

American Lieutenant Colonel James L. Kincaid, Provincial Commissioner, Naples Province, of the Allied Control Commission, realized that a major eruption of Vesuvius would not only disrupt the already devastated metropolitan area but would hinder military operations. The morning after Imbo and Drake's expedition, Kincaid drove with Lieutenant Colonel John A. Warner up past the observatory and stopped his Jeep in front of the lava flow. They estimated that the flow was now five hundred feet wide, twelve feet high and advancing at a speed of fifteen feet per hour.

The slow-moving mass seemed to offer no immediate danger to San Sebastiano. Nevertheless, Kincaid returned to his headquarters where he began drawing contingency plans in the event the eruption worsened. He was abruptly awakened at 1:25 Monday morning, March 20, with the news that San Sebastiano was indeed in danger. He drove to the village and set up a command headquarters at the iron bridge that separated the town from its sister community, Massa di Somma.

Trust in God and in the Allied Control Commission was all the people of San Sebastiano had that morning when Vesuvius exploded again, sending a new river of lava aimed directly at their town. Under Kincaid's direction, the U.S. Army evacuated the civilians, completing the task by the next night even as the lava arrived at the edge of town to bury San Sebastiano for the fourth time in 122 years.

After San Sebastiano and Massa di Somma were engulfed, the lava flow from Vesuvius slowed perceptibly. Yet Professor Imbo's seismographs at the observatory recorded continuing activity within the volcano. Vesuvius was building strength for another assault.

It came at 5:15 the afternoon of March 22, 1944. There was no effusion of lava, but this time the volcano erupted in a cascade of dark gray dust, gas and molten ash in the form of a mushroom cloud. The debris was driven upward to a height of twenty thousand feet, a black mantle torn apart by lightning, followed by thunder. At the rate of a half million cubic yards per hour, the ash disgorged from the mountain, bringing a premature darkness to the region. Controlled by the prevailing winds, the path of the ash could not be predicted with the same probability as a lava flow. Villages to the south and east previously spared by the lava eruption now suffered a volcanic deluge.

All night, black lapilli, small airborne volcanic stones, assailed the Campanian countryside. The weight of falling stones accumulated on rooftops and snapped the support beams, collapsing homes upon their inhabitants. A portion of the roof fell in at the 103d General Hospital at Nocera, but the wounded Allied soldiers had already been evacuated. The church dome in the same village toppled.

The countryside woke to the sight of a black blizzard with ash and sooty lapilli piled up as high as four feet. Like soiled snow, the debris drifted, blocking roads and smothering the early crops of farmers. An Allied airfield had to be closed because of obstructed runways. Convoys were halted as Jeeps became bogged in soft ash as high as their hubcaps.

In the end, the suffocating ash had killed more people than the lava. Twelve died in Nocera, nine more at Pagani. Falling fragments killed three people in Terzigno. Counting two boys killed by an exploding well in San Sebastiano, the death toll was twenty-six.

As I sat listening to Giuseppe Imbo, now eighty years old, tell his story of the 1944 eruption, I began to think of the millions of people who gamble their lives daily against the chance that Vesuvius might claim them. Many have not rested easily since the 1980 earthquake, which fractured the earth so close to the crossing faultlines that mark the vent of their volcano. Was it, indeed, a seismic portent eerily similar to the great earthquake preceding the eruption that destroyed Pompeii and Herculaneum?

I wondered about the present level of danger. Addressing the man who has been intimately associated with the volcano longer than anyone alive, I asked: "Is Vesuvius dead?"

"No," he replied sharply. "In 1964 the bottom of the crater lowered. Collapses like that preceded many eruptions in the past, including the one in 1906. As the magma tries to work its way up through the blocked vent, it fuses the rock above it, creating pockets of space that make the crater slowly fall in. Between 1970 and 1974 the crater bottom lowered about five feet. The longer the process continues, the greater the pressure that is brought to bear on the magma chamber."

I then asked Imbo the ultimate question: "When will Vesuvius erupt again?"

The professor pondered. The eruption of 1944 was obviously a classic paroxysmal explosion that had ended a Vesuvian cycle, he explained. Based upon Palmieri's thesis there should have been a resumption of mild activity in the 1950s culminating in a grand explosion that has yet to come. If we consider that the last two eruptions, 1906 and 1944, were spaced thirty-eight years apart, simple arithmetic leads to a riveting conclusion.

But Imbo cautioned me. Geological events are difficult to

predict over short periods. He searched among the papers on his desk, producing a 1979 study from the *Journal of the Italian Society of Mineralology and Petrology*. In it, scientists document a seventeen-thousand-year Vesuvian pattern that is divided into eight cycles of roughly two thousand years. Each of these cycles has begun with an enormous Pompeiian-type eruption.

The scientists see two possible scenarios for the future of Vesuvius and the people of Campania. If the 1944 eruption was the culmination of one of these long-term cycles, then Vesuvius could remain quiet for some time before exploding again in an awesome eruption the size of the one that buried Pompeii.

But if Vesuvius is somewhere in the middle of one of the long cycles, the scientists believe that the volcano will begin a renewal of its activity "at any time" causing an eruption of "unforeseeable energy."

Professor Imbo laid the paper face down on his coffee table and looked at me intently, as if to underscore the point. "The volcano is never dead," he affirmed quietly. "Vesuvius lives."

Soon after the eruption of 1906, the *New York Times* commented editorially on Vesuvius and the stubborn nature of the people who inhabit its slopes. Their words proved to be prophetic. "Only this is sure," said the *Times*. "The sides and neighborhood of Vesuvius will be inhabited until the very last habitability, and, even if the great devastation comes, people will go creeping back afterward. . . ."

The date of that great devastation-to-come is not known, but little has changed since 1906, or 1944. The people of Campania, like a microcosm of all that is indomitable in humanity, cling tenaciously to the slopes of their feared and loved neighbor and await the next eruption just as they have done since the days of Pompeii.

BIBLIOGRAPHY

Allied Control Commission Headquarters Naples Province. *Final Report on the Vesuvius Emergency Operation.* Naples: 1944.

Annual Report of the Board of Regents of the Smithsonian Institution, 1909. Washington, D.C.: 1910.

Ashby, T. "Herculaneum." *Independent* 63:21–25.

Auldjo, John. *Sketches of Vesuvius.* London: Longman, Rees, Orme, Brown, Green and Longman, 1833.

Babbage, Charles. *Passages from the Life of a Philosopher.* London: Dawsons of Pall Mall, 1968.

Barker, Ethel Ross. *Buried Herculaneum.* London: Adam and Charles Black, 1908.

Bellicard, Mr. *Observations Upon the Antiquities of the Town of Herculaneum, Discovered at the Foot of Mount Vesuvius.* London: D. Wilson and T. Durham, 1753.

Bennett, Henry Grey. "Account of the Ancient Rolls of Papyrus, Discovered at Herculaneum . . ." *Archaeologia,* vol. 15, 1802.

Berkeley, Edward. "Extract of a Letter from Mr. Edward Berkeley at Naples, Giving Several Curious Observations and Remarks on the Eruptions of Fire and Smoke from Mount Vesuvius." *Philosophical Transactions of the Royal Society of London,* vol. XXX.

Bonney, T. G. *Volcanoes: Their Structure and Significance.* London: John Murray, 1899.

Carrington, R. C. *Pompeii.* Oxford: Clarendon Press, 1936.

Clarke, William. *Pompeii.* Boston: Lilly, Wait, Coleman and Holden, 1833.

Clemens, Samuel L. (Mark Twain). *The Innocents Abroad or The New Pilgrims' Progress.* Hartford: American Publishing Co., 1875.

Corti, Egon Caesar Conte. *The Destruction and Resurrection of Pompeii and Herculaneum.* Munich: F. Bruckmann, 1940.

d'Aragona, N. M. "On the Eruption of Vesuvius, in May 1737." *Philosophical Transactions of the Royal Society of London,* vol. XLI.

Daubeny, Charles. *A Description of Active and Extinct Volcanoes, of Earthquakes, and of Thermal Springs.* 2nd ed. London: Richard and John E. Taylor, 1848.

deCoulanges, Numa Denis Fustel. *The Ancient City: A Study on the Religion, Laws, and Institutions of Greece and Rome.* New York: Doubleday Anchor, 1873.

de Franciscis, Alfonso. *The National Archaeological Museum of Naples.* Naples: Interdipress, 1974.

Dickens, Charles. *Pictures From Italy, And American Notes for General Circulation.* New York: Hurd and Houghton, 1877.

Drummond, William, and Walpole, Robert. *Herculanensia: Or Archaeological and Philological Dissertations, containing a Manuscript Found Among the Ruins of Herculaneum.* London: W. Bulmer, 1810.

Ellaby, C. G. *Pompeii and Herculaneum.* London: Methuen and Co., 1930.

Engelmann, Richard. *Pompeii.* Translated by Talfourd Ely. London: H. Grecel, 1904.

"Extracts of Two Letters to Thomas Hollis concerning the late Discoveries at Herculaneum." *Philosophical Transactions of the Royal Society of London,* vol. XLIX.

Foster, Herbert Baldwin, trans. *Dio's Rome.* New York: Pafraets, 1906.

Gell, Sir William. *Pompeiana: The Topography, Edifices, and Ornaments of Pompeii.* 2nd. ed. London: Rodwell and Martin, 1821.

Grant, Michael. *Cities of Vesuvius: Pompeii and Herculaneum.* New York: Macmillan, 1971.

Hamilton, H. C. and Falconer, W., trans. *The Geography of Strabo.* London: George Bell and Sons, 1892.

Hamilton, Sir William. "Account of the Discoveries at Pompeii." *Archaeologia* 4: 159–61.

———. "An Account of the Late Eruption of Mount Vesuvius." *Philosophical Transactions of the Royal Society of London,* vol. LXXXV.

———. *Campi Phlegrai.* Naples: 1776.

———. "Further Particulars on Mount Vesuvius . . ." *Philosophical Transactions of the Royal Society of London,* vol. LIX.

———. "On the Eruption of Mount Vesuvius in August 1779 . . ." *Philosophical Transactions of the Royal Society of London,* vol. LXX.

———. "On the Eruption of Mount Vesuvius in 1767 . . ." *Philosophical Transactions of the Royal Society of London,* vol. LVIII.

———. "Some Particulars of the Present State of Mount Vesuvius . . ." *Philosophical Transactions of the Royal Society of London,* vol. LXXVI.

———. "Two Letters to Envoy Extraordinary at Naples, Containing an Account of the Last Eruption of Mount Vesuvius . . ." *Philo-*

sophical Transactions of the Royal Society of London, vol. LVII.

Hulbert, Charles. *Volcanic Wonders, And Scenes of Astonishment: Being Historic and Scientific Descriptions of the Volcanoes of the Azores, and a General View of Burning Mountains, In Various Parts of the Globe.* London: C. Hulbert, 1827.

Iddings, Joseph P. *The Problem of Volcanism.* New Haven: Yale University Press, 1894.

Jashemski, Wilhelmina F. "The Discovery of a Large Vineyard at Pompeii: University of Maryland Excavations, 1970." Reprint: *American Journal of Archaeology*, vol. 77, January 1973.

Johnson, Helgi, and Smith, Bennett L., eds. *The Megatectonics of Continents and Oceans.* New Brunswick, N.J.: Rutgers University Press, 1970.

Judd, John W. *Volcanoes: What They Are and What They Teach.* New York: D. Appleton, 1881.

la Condamine, Mons. "Extract of a Letter . . ." *Philosophical Transactions of the Royal Society of London*, vol. XLIX.

Lacroix, A. "The Eruption of Vesuvius in April 1906." *Smithsonian Report*, 1906.

Leppman, Wolfgang. *Pompeii in Fact and Fiction.* London: Elek Books, 1966.

Lobley, J. Logan. *Mount Vesuvius: A Descriptive, Historical, and Geological Account of the Volcano and Its Surroundings.* London: Roper and Drowley, 1889.

Lyell, Sir Charles. *Principles of Geology.* Vol. 1. New York: Johnson Reprint, 1969.

Lytton, Lord. *The Last Days of Pompeii.* London: Thomas Nelson and Sons, 1834.

Macchioro, Vittorio. *The Villa of the Mysteries.* Naples: American and British Club, Mary E. Raiola, c. 1920.

Maiuri, Amedeo. *Herculaneum.* Translated by V. Priestley. Instituto Poligrafico Dello Stato, 1959.

Marriott, H. P. FitzGerald. *Facts About Pompeii: Its Masons' Marks, Town Walls, Houses, and Portraits.* London: Hazell, Watson and Viney, 1895.

Mau, August. "Mau's Pompeii." *The Nation* 69:450–51.

Melmoth, William, trans. "The Eruption of Vesuvius as Described in the Letters of Pliny." *Chautauguan* 4:157–61.

Nepos, Cornelius. *Lucius Annaeus Florus: Epitome of Roman History.* London: William Heinemann, 1929.

"Of the Eruption of Mount Vesuvius in October 1751 . . ." *Philosophical Transactions of the Royal Society of London*, vol. XLVII.

Oldfather, C. H., trans. *Diodorus of Sicily.* Cambridge, Mass.: Harvard University Press, 1935.

Ordinaire, M. *The Natural History of Volcanoes: Including Subma-*

rine Volcanoes, and Other Analogous Phenomena. Translated by R. C. Dallas. London: Cadell, Jun. and Davis, 1801.

Paderni, Camillo. "Extracts of two letters . . ." *Philosophical Transactions of the Royal Society of London,* vol. XLI.

Palmieri, Luigi. *The Eruption of Vesuvius in 1872.* London: Asher and Co., 1873.

Parker, John. "Part of a letter from Mr. John Parker to his father at London, concerning the late eruption of Mount Vesuvius, dated Rome, Dec. 20 . . ." *Philosophical Transactions of the Royal Society of London,* vol. XLIV.

Perret, Frank A. *Volcanological Observations.* Washington, D.C.: Carnegie Institution of Washington, 1950.

———. *The Vesuvius Eruption of 1906.* Washington, D.C.: Carnegie Institution of Washington, 1924.

Phillips, John. *Vesuvius.* Oxford: Clarendon Press, 1864.

Plinius, Secundus C. *Pliny's Natural History: An Account by a Roman of What Romans Knew and Did and Valued.* Compiled by Loyd Haberly. New York: Frederick Ungar, 1957.

Plutarch. *Plutarch's Lives.* Edited by John S. White. New York: Biblo & Tannen, 1900.

Pompeii A.D. 79. Vols. I and II. Boston: The Museum of Fine Arts, 1978.

Pompeii As Source and Inspiration: Reflections in Eighteenth and Nineteenth Century Art. Ann Arbor, Mich.: University of Michigan Museum of Art, 1977.

Procopius of Caesarea. Translated by H. B. Dewing. London: William Heinemann, 1919.

Radice, Betty. *The Letters of the Younger Pliny.* New York: Penguin, 1975.

Ramage, T. C. "Account of Excavations made at Pompeii from December 1826 to August 1827." *Edinburgh Philosophical Journal* 4:244–51.

Rittmann, Alfred. *Volcanoes and Their Activity.* Translated by E. A. Vincent. New York: John Wiley and Sons, 1962.

Shelley, Percy Bysshe. *Essays and Letters.* London: Walter Scott, 1886.

Skurray, Wickes. *A Description of the First Discoveries of the Ancient City of Heraclea.* London: R. Baldwin, 1750.

Sloane, William. "Discovery of the remains of a city under-ground, near Naples . . ." *Philosophical Transactions of the Royal Society of London,* vol. XLI.

Stiles, Sir Francis Haskins Eyles. "Account of an Eruption of Mount Vesuvius." *Philosophical Transactions of the Royal Society of London,* vol. LII.

Tacitus, Cornelius. *The Complete Works of Tacitus.* Translated by Alfred J. Church and William Hackson Brodribb. New York: The Modern Library.

Tanzer, Helen H. *The Common People of Pompeii, A Study of the Graffiti.* Baltimore: Johns Hopkins Press, 1939.

Trevelyan, Raleigh. *The Shadow of Vesuvius.* London: Joseph, 1976.

Valetta, S. "An Account of the Eruption of Mount Vesuvius in 1707." *Philosophical Transactions of the Royal Society of London,* vol. XXVIII.

"Vesuvius." *Life,* April 17, 1944.

Walston, Charles. *Herculaneum, Past, Present and Future.* London: Macmillan and Co., 1908.

Winckelmann, Johann J. *Writings On Art.* London: Phaidon, 1972.